The *One* Rule
For Boys

How Empathy And Emotional Understanding Will Improve Just About Everything For Your Son

DR. MAX WACHTEL

FriesenPress

Suite 300 – 990 Fort Street
Victoria, BC, Canada V8W 1H8
www.friesenpress.com

**Copyright © 2014 by
Maximillian Wachtel, Ph.D. LLC dba Cherry Creek Press**
First Edition — 2014

www.oneruleforboys.com
www.maxwachtel.com

ISBN
978-1-4602-4722-8 (Hardcover)
978-1-4602-4723-5 (Paperback)
978-1-4602-4724-2 (eBook)

1. Family & Relationships, Child Care

Distributed to the trade by The Ingram Book Company

TABLE OF CONTENTS

CHAPTER 1

Boys Will Be Boys: introduction

When I was in the fifth grade, I killed a turtle.

That's a bit harsh—actually it was an accident. But I might have been able to stop it, had I known how to deal with tricky emotional situations.

Here is what happened: I was on the playground with five other boys. One of them caught a turtle before school started. As boys, it was only natural that we were interested. I mean, it was a turtle.

We were playing good-naturedly with the animal when two of the boys became aggressive. What would happen if we poke it with a stick? Can we whack it on the shell? Let's flip it over and watch it squirm.

I was uncomfortable, but I was a quiet kid. Being the only Jewish kid in the small-town, northern Wyoming school I attended taught me that being different was uncomfortable. I didn't say anything—even though I knew what we were doing was wrong. I didn't want to make waves with my friends and get called out once again for being different. Besides, what would I have said? I had no idea what to do, so I stayed quiet and felt horribly guilty.

Then the aggression got out of hand. One of the wrongdoers decided to send the turtle down the playground slide. Keep in mind, this was the early 1980s. Safety standards for playground equipment was quite a bit more lax back then. The slide was about 35 feet high,[1] and it was steep. I've never heard a story about a kid dying on one of those slides, but ours was the site of several broken bones and at least one bloody tongue.[2]

The kid climbed to the top of the slide and let the turtle go. It picked up a lot of speed as it descended.[3] Then it flew off the end and smacked onto the ground. As it slowly scrambled, trying to get away, another boy retrieved it and ushered it back to the top. This happened again and again.

On the fourth trip down the slide, the turtle flipped over and landed on its back. One of the boys picked it up, and we all saw that its shell had cracked. We looked at it in silence. Even the lead wrongdoer was quiet.

Then the bell rang.

We needed to get in line and go to class. None of us knew what to do, but we suspected we would get in trouble if we brought an injured turtle into the school.[4]

The only solution was to leave the turtle behind. One of the boys carried it to a grassy area and set it down. We went to class. We didn't speak of the turtle for the rest of the day. In fact, I don't remember saying anything to anyone about it ever again.

I am not sure what happened to the turtle, but—realistically—it probably slowly crawled somewhere and died shortly thereafter. I

---

[1] This may be a slight exaggeration.

[2] If you don't know what I am talking about, try sticking your tongue on something metal when it is below freezing outside. See what happens. Make sure you have plenty of time. You will be there for a while.

[3] Do you remember those high school physics equations that dealt with frictionless planes? They were based on this slide.

[4] Especially since we had caused that injury.

felt horrible about what I had done. Actually, I hadn't *done* anything, and that was part of the problem. I didn't torture the turtle, but I didn't stop its torture either. I knew that sending it down the slide over and over again was a bad idea, but I didn't say anything.

I don't know why this turtle story has stuck with me for so many years. Maybe because it was so out of character for me. I did not torture animals. I was the kid who found the injured bird and carried it for two miles to the veterinary clinic, not the kid who cracked shells and left animals to die. In my mind, only bad kids did that. Interestingly, my instinct to stay away from kids who were cruel to animals was spot on. Boys who intentionally hurt animals are likely to engage in anger-induced illegal behavior later in life.[5] The callousness and lack of emotion necessary to hurt a defenseless animal is an excellent predictor of future criminal offending in young men.[6]

There is a good reason for me to remember that turtle. Looking back on it, I realize I was ill-equipped to deal with such a complicated emotional situation. My parents did as good a job of raising me as they could, but I did not learn to recognize my emotions, regulate them, and think critically through tough situations until much later in life. In fact, I was highly rewarded for ignoring my emotions as a child. I was a ball of anxiety, sadness, and anger for much of my childhood, but I learned to hide those emotions well. Teachers, my parents, and my friends' parents all complimented me on how calm and unaffected I was. I was unshakable. Nothing bothered me. I felt great pride in my stoicism.

But on the inside, I felt a tremendous amount of turmoil. It took years to figure out how to untangle my emotions and learn to appropriately express myself. Instead of continuing to pretend everything was fine, I forced myself to confront my emotions, understand them, and express them in appropriate ways. It was

---

[5] Lucia & Killias (2011)
[6] Kahn, et al. (2013)

a liberating feeling. Instead of only feeling anger or anxiety, I started experiencing a wide range of so-called *negative* emotions. I was able to express them appropriately, and so they started to dissipate. Instead of two options—either pushing it all down or letting it all out uncontrollably— I gave myself a host of potential reactions I could have to tough situations.

I am grateful I figured out how to recognize and regulate my emotions, and it has helped me tremendously in my life. I am certain I am a better person as a result, and I know it has helped my career. But I learned those skills as an adult, and partially by accident. Boys are not taught to do these things, and it holds them back. Many never learn. The ones who do learn those skills do so despite society telling them that is not how *real men* behave.

I wish someone had taught me to do this as a kid—to recognize and regulate my emotions and to understand the emotions of others. To be fair to the adults in my life though, I was a tough nut to crack. I pushed my emotions down so far that it was impossible to tell how I was feeling. I am pretty sure my go-to facial expression was slightly less animated than that of a mannequin. My parents and teachers did the best job they could, given what I gave them to work with.

Most kids are not as emotionally inexpressive as I was though. Usually, when a boy is feeling anxious or angry, everyone around him knows something is wrong. He gets into trouble at home and school. His grades drop. He fights. He loses friends. He picks the wrong friends. He might even hurt animals. When left unattended, those uncontrolled feelings and behaviors can cause a lot of problems. Some kids grow out of it on their own—thank goodness[7]—but a lot of angry boys turn into angry men. Most angry men make life

---

[7] Researchers don't exactly know why this is, but some kids merely get over things. They mature and stop behaving badly for no apparent reason.

less enjoyable for those around them, and often pass that anger along to their children like a poisoned family heirloom.[8]

Angry men are a real problem for society

In 2008, men were seven times more likely to commit murder than women. When a woman is a victim of homicide, her intimate partner is the killer 41.5% of the time.[9] From 1995 through 2010, 2.1 out of every 1000 women in the U.S. had been sexually assaulted. In other words, a woman's chance of being sexually assaulted by a man during that time-frame was 1 in 476.[10] By contrast, that same woman's chance of dying by getting run over by a car when crossing the street was about 1 in 749.[11] It was more dangerous to hang around a man than to cross the street.

In addition, about 55% of sexual assaults from 2005-2010 took place at or near the woman's home. 78% of the time, the woman knew her male attacker. 34% of the time, it was her male intimate partner.[12] 1 in every 256 women in the U.S. was the victim of some type of male-initiated domestic violence in 2009.[13] *Most male domestic abusers are both angry and clinically depressed.*[14]

The good news in all of the above statistics is that violent crime rates have dropped substantially in the past two decades. But it is still alarming that—according to the National Safety Council—the following are the five most dangerous activities in which a woman can engage, from most to least dangerous:[15]

---

[8] Barry & Kochanska (2010)
[9] Cooper & Smith (2011)
[10] Planty & Langton (2013)
[11] Injury Facts (2013)
[12] Planty & Langton (2013)
[13] Truman & Rand (2010)
[14] Maiuro, et al. (1988)
[15] Injury Facts (2013)

1. Intentionally harming herself (for example, attempting suicide)

2. Riding in a car

3. Accidentally exposing herself to noxious substances (like carbon monoxide)

4. Falling

5. Living with a man

So yes, angry men are a problem, and the most surprising thing about these statistics is that we, as a society, do this to our boys. We train boys to be unemotional. We teach them that crying is for sissies. We show them example after example of men solving problems through conflict. We tell them that men who have empathy for others are weak.

When a boy is loud, rambunctious, athletic, strong, and aggressive, we say he is *all boy*. Even though quiet, empathic, sensitive boys are technically *all boy* as well, we don't think of them in those terms. We think of them as having feminine qualities, and assume that those qualities are weaker than the *all boy*, masculine qualities.

We also say, "*Let boys be boys.*"

What we are really saying is, "*Let boys behave badly.*"

When we say "Let boys be boys," what we mean is, "*Boys are aggressive. They are mean. They will behave badly.*" But none of that is inherently true. When boys are taught how to express their emotions properly, and to understand the emotions of others, they don't explode in rage. They don't solve their problems with anger. They don't behave badly. And they are still *all boy*.

Think back to the turtle story. There were a number of ways I could have resolved the situation, and it would have ended differently. I chose to do nothing and the turtle died. There *were* other options.

I could have yelled at the boys. I could have fought them. I could have pushed them out of the way and taken the turtle by force. I could have begged them to stop. I could have tried kindly asking them. I could have cried. I could have walked away.

To be honest, I don't think any of those options would have helped much. Some would not have worked at all. Some would have saved the turtle's life. Some would have made the boys very angry, and so I would have needed to deal with their revenge at a later time. None of those options would have left me feeling like I had any power over the situation.

It's all about power and control

Power. That is what it is about. Men[16] want to be in control. They want to be powerful. They want respect. But they are socialized to go after it in the wrong ways. They are taught that if you hold back your emotions, you have power over them. If you are physically intimidating, you command respect. If you shoot first and ask questions later, you are a take-charge kind of guy.

That is the attitude that permeates our culture, and it crosses all racial, ethnic, and socioeconomic backgrounds. Boys walk into school and shoot for revenge. They drive their cars by strangers' houses and shoot for respect. They tease kids who are different. They bully kids who are weak. They learn to constrict their negative emotions so tightly that only anger and anxiety are allowed to escape.

In an ironic twist of fate, we attempt to teach boys to be powerful and in control by socializing them in ways that actually strip away their power and control. But what if there was another possibility? One that gives boys permission to feel and regulate their emotions, to understand others, and to use those skills to make

---

16 People really, not just men.

the world a better place?[17] *That* would be real power. *That* would be raising boys to be in control of their lives. And it would teach them to use that power and control for good.

There is a better way

Going back to the turtle story again, imagine a scenario where I reacted by punching the lead tormenter and ripping the turtle out of his hands. Justice would have been served, but at a cost. I would have learned that violence is an appropriate way to resolve a problem, and the other boy and his friends would have been angry with me. I would have felt righteous and victorious, and I would have had to deal with the other boys' bad feelings at a later time—most likely through more violence. I would have had no idea how the other boys were feeling or what motivated them to torture the turtle in the first place.

But what if I had been able to recognize what I was feeling at the time—guilt, shame, frustration, and fear— *and* been able to understand where the lead tormenter was coming from? Maybe he was being abused at home. Maybe other kids were bullying him, and he was acting out his frustration on an innocent creature.[18] Maybe he was a little sociopath in the making. If I could truly understand the boy's feelings and motivation, I would have been better equipped to react appropriately. I could have talked to him about how it is wrong to hurt an animal just because he was being hurt, or I could have helped him go to a teacher and report the bullying problem, or I could have known to walk away from him and never play with him again because nothing was going to help.

I would have been able to experience my emotions and come up with a plan of action. I would have been able to make good

---

[17] Spoiler alert: There is another way, and it is outlined in this book.

[18] This is a defense mechanism known as *displacement*.

decisions about how to react in a socially appropriate way. I would have been able to understand which boys were worth befriending and which I should avoid. I may not have saved the turtle, but I would have felt powerful. I would have been in control.

This is my motivation to write this book. I want to help parents and educators teach boys the skills they need to be strong leaders in what is a very cold world. We equate rudeness with power.[19] We give others a free pass (and a whole lot of power) when they break the rules.[20] Politics has become a blood sport.[21] Social media and the Internet have become places to berate strangers with angry tirades.[22] Countries go to war.[23] Violent crime occurs.[24] The list goes on and on.

Instead of the status quo, I'd like to be able to say, *"Let boys be boys,"* and mean, *"Let boys experience a full range of emotions, understand others, and develop into productive, 21st century leaders."*

The one rule for boys

<u>Understand your own emotions, regulate those emotions, and have empathy for others.</u>[25]

As you will learn in future chapters, the three skills listed above are all tied to empathy. If boys are able to understand and have empathy for themselves, they will be able to better regulate their emotions and understand the motivations of others. It all starts with empathy.

---

[19] Van Kleef, et al. (2011)
[20] Van Kleef, et al. (2012)
[21] Do I really need a citation for this one?
[22] Wolchover (2012)
[23] For more information on this phenomenon, please reference the world's entire written history.
[24] See above citations on crime statistics.
[25] Already, that sounds like three rules.

So is this one rule—having empathy—enough? Of course not. There are many important rules for boys. They need to go to school, put on pants, lower the toilet seat, learn the importance of paying rent ... just to name a few. But empathy is a big one. As you continue reading, you will begin to understand how that one rule—an empathic outlook—can help a boy understand why school, pants, toilet seats, and rent are important rules to follow as well.[26]

And even if living in an empathic manner were the most important rule for boys, which is a claim no psychologist can make, it is easier said than done. That is why I have broken down the *one rule* in this book into many action steps and hundreds of tips.[27]

A major caveat: most boys aren't all that bad

Most parents do a good job of raising their boys to be responsible men. Although men are the cause of most of the world's crime, wars, aggression, and so forth, most men do not commit crimes. Most don't start wars. Most are not overly aggressive.

But the fact remains that we still have crime, war, and aggression. Society still has too many men who behave badly. And it is the responsibility of each of us to change that. Let's take our good boys and make them great. Let's allow our boys to be *all boy* in the truest sense—fully experiencing the human condition in a way that allows them to be empathic, fair, assertive, and powerful.

Along with a good number of girls, those empathic boys are the ones who will rise to become society's new generation of leaders, lifting everyone up with them and improving the world.

---

[26] Plus, the title *One Rule, Of Many, On Which You Should Focus To Improve Boys' Lives While They Also Learn The Importance Of Wearing Pants* was already taken.
[27] And by hundreds, I mean almost one hundred.

Working with criminals has made me want to help boys

My doctoral training is in counseling psychology, and for the last ten years, I have worked primarily as a forensic psychologist. I work with criminals. Mostly men. I conduct assessments for the courts, including competency and sanity evaluations, risk evaluations, and pre-sentence, mental-health evaluations. I work with attorneys to help them understand their clients' motivations so that they can explain those motivations to judges and juries. I spend a lot of time thinking about the worst issues of humanity— murder, sexual assault, child abuse, and armed robbery, to name just a few.

I also work at a television station, where I analyze the psychological aspects of the day's news stories. Although I try to focus on positive topics, a lot of what I work on in this arena tends to be negative. Crime, politics,[28] poor parenting, severe mental illness, addiction, and psychopathy.

In addition to my other work, I taught at a university for 12 years,[29] where I focused on diagnosing psychopathology and the myriad legal and ethical problems associated with the field of psychology.

To sum up—all of the coldness in the world? I focus on that for a living.

You might think it is a stretch for someone with my background to be writing a book that helps boys. But keep in mind, the criminals with whom I work came from somewhere. They were all boys once. In fact, some of them are barely out of their childhood before heading down the long road of lifelong incarceration.

---

[28] If you don't think politics is a largely negative enterprise, you might not be paying close enough attention.

[29] Full disclosure: If you view my Linked In profile, it accurately calculates my tenure at the university at 11 years, 11 months. To make myself sound better, I round up.

Almost all of these men, regardless of age, are emotionally immature[30]—thinking there are only two options in life: React with anger or don't react at all. Suck it up. Be a man. Don't cry. Fight for what is yours.

The Turtle

I don't think any of the kids who hurt the turtle on my elementary school playground ended up in prison, but I still think back to that day and wonder how differently we all might have turned out if the adults in our lives had been able to teach us how to think about our emotions, regulate them, have empathy toward other beings, and deal with difficult situations. The overwhelming amount of psychological research points to one simple conclusion: Those are the skills boys need in order to be happy, have better friends, find success at work, and become the type of leaders who elevate society and make the world a better place.

And that is the goal of this book—to help parents and educators teach boys the skills necessary to live happy, productive lives, to treat others with the kindness they deserve, and to solve problems responsibly. I want a world filled with boys and men who know what is right and who can reflect on their own experiences to better understand the worldview of others. I want men who respect women. I want men who strive to treat everyone equitably. I want to empower adults to raise responsible boys who will embody humanity at its best. Worst case scenario, I would at the very least like to teach boys how to avoid engaging in the types of activities that lead to prison.[31] Best case, I would like to teach parents how to raise content and strong boys who improve the world.

---

[30] Hartnett & Shumate (1980); Mackinnon (1988)
[31] My original admittedly negative and condescending title for this book was *How To Raise Boys Who Don't Kill*.

I want parents and educators to take good boys and make them great. I want them to *let boys be boys*. I want them to raise boys who are *all boy*.

Men mess things up, but this book can help change that

In addition to witnessing the problems associated with criminal offenders, I have noticed over the years that men tend to cause most of the world's problems.[32] Men start wars. Men tell women what they can and cannot do. Men argue with each other in Congress and nothing gets done. We, as men, also do amazing things—we send rockets to the moon, we create vaccines for deadly diseases, we take sports and turn them into multi-billion dollar industries. But at our worst, we mess things up. Badly.

Men don't have to mess up the world, though. We can raise a generation of mighty boys who grow into responsible, productive, and empathic men. In order to do that, I will address a number of issues. In Chapter 2, I explain the concept of reflective thinking and use that concept to examine some of the common explanations as to why boys have problems with anger and emotional expression. Chapter 3 goes into more detail about how socializing boys in different ways can help reduce the risk of a number of emotional and behavioral problems.

Chapter 4 gets into the meat of the book. In this chapter, I teach parents how to recognize, understand, and regulate their own emotions. If you are having a problem with this yourself, it will be extremely difficult to teach your boys how to do it. In Chapter 5, I cover research-based teaching practices you can use as you teach these new skills to your boys, and in Chapter 6, I outline the entire process and provide sample wording for you to

---

[32] To be fair, I don't think it takes a Ph.D. in psychology to recognize this.

use in specific situations with your boys. Finally, in Chapter 7, I cover what to do if the techniques in this book are not working.

Research-based: but practical in its application

In writing this book, it was important to me that I not waste the readers' time with my personal opinions. I like to think I have good common sense, and I generally know enough about psychology to make good educated guesses about the best ways to raise boys. But one of the central tenets of this book is to encourage boys to think critically and reflectively and to make good decisions based on that thinking. It would be hypocritical of me to tell you how to think based on information I am making up.

In order to avoid that issue, I have consulted psychological research. I do not make any important claims or suggestions that are not based on peer-reviewed literature. In most cases, I have tried to use the most recent research available. If you look at the reference section, you will see that most of the citations have been published within the last ten years.[33] There are exceptions of course—some phenomena I cover have been researched long ago, and I've cited some classic psychological studies from earlier in the last century. But by and large, I have tried to keep the book current.

I also want the book to be a practical guide. As much as I would like readers to carefully study each chapter, reading them several times and absorbing all of the material (and encouraging their friends to do the same) I understand how real life works. For those of you who want to do so, I encourage you to read the book several times and pick up every small nuance of my argument. For the rest of you, I have added numerous tips throughout my chapters

---

[33] This, of course, assumes that the book is less than 10 years old when you are reading it. If it is 2024 or beyond as you are reading this, I recommend you either find the most recent edition of this book or do something else with your time.

so that, after reading the book once, you can pick it up, open it to almost any page, and quickly remind yourself of a way you can put the suggested techniques into immediate, practical use.

The Turtle, again

That poor turtle. In the grand scheme of my life, the little creature made almost no difference to me. If we had played with it, let it go, and watched it crawl away to safety, my life would be no different than it is today. If I had stood up for the turtle when my friend started messing with it, I'm not sure my life would be any different, either. It is sad to think how little its life and death meant to me. It was just one small episode in a life filled with much bigger moments.

And that is the way it is for all boys. Life is filled with those small moments, most of which we don't even consciously recall. Any one of them means almost nothing to us. But added together, it is those small moments that shape who we are and the men we become. Wouldn't it be nice if we could teach boys to confront those small moments with confidence, empathy, and thoughtful reflection, so that they could break out of the shells that otherwise limit their choices to inaction or anger?[34] Wouldn't it be nice if those small moments could shape all boys' lives in ways that help them grow into great men who improve the world?

Let's let our boys be boys, in the fullest sense of that phrase. Let's allow them to be *all boy*, as opposed to the limited version of boyhood to which we currently restrict them.

---

[34] Did you see what I did there? Turtles have shells...remember the turtle? We put unnecessary shells on our boys, too.

CHAPTER 2

Why Some Boys Go Bad: using reflective
thinking to understand the problem

Without boys, the world would be a safer place. There would be considerably less violence. Less crime. Less anger. Less war. What with modern science, women could probably even figure out how to procreate without men.[35]

But the world would be so much worse without boys. There would be less competition. Fewer challenges of authority. Less chance of reaching the bowl on the top shelf. There would probably be no baseball. No testosterone.[36] No boys to grow into men. No dads to hug their sons, to patch up their scraped knees, and to teach them how to treat others. Star Wars and Lego might not exist. We might not have felt compelled to fly to the moon. Let's face it—women *would* have accomplished some of these same feats, and they probably would have done other equally

---

[35] However, since they do not have the genetic material to create boys, in a few generations the planet could be populated completely by women. Guys, keep this in mind the next time you start badmouthing a woman—she has the power to wipe out your gender.

[36] To be more accurate, there would be *less* testosterone, as it is a hormone that naturally occurs in both men and women.

impressive stuff, but there is no doubt that a boy's passion, developed into a man's ability, has the potential to improve the world in dramatic ways—for the better or the worse.

Ridding the world of boys is not a viable option, and even if it were, it would be a horrible tragedy. But the fact still remains that boys are sometimes a problem. That is what this chapter is about—trying to determine why this is the case.

Throughout the years, a number of common themes have emerged in an attempt to explain why people go bad. This chapter will cover some of the most common explanations, and use critical, reflective thinking to dissect those issues. Clinical research will be used to gain a deeper understanding, and the results may be surprising in some cases.

Research shows that some of the theoretical reasons why boys go bad are flat-out wrong. Others are right. In most cases, however, the research is mixed. Let me offer a word of warning: Reflective thinking is an emotionally difficult exercise, and the following sections may be a challenge for you. Some will confirm what you already believe. But other sections will not. They may cause you to experience anxiety, or anger, or disbelief. During those times, it is important for you to reflect on *why* you are having the emotional reaction you are having. It won't always be easy, but confronting your deeply held beliefs is an important aspect of growing as a human. And after all, you will be asking your boys to do some tough stuff too.

Here is another word of warning: You are not the perfect parent. No one is. And that is not a problem. Our society is doing reasonably well at the moment, with everyone graggling through. Most of us raise boys who turn into fine men. The goal of this chapter is not to make you feel bad about your parenting abilities. It is not to teach you how to be the perfect parent. The goal is to help you gain an understanding of where some of the problem areas are in raising boys so we can take our good-parenting techniques and make them great.

Reflective thinking: an important skill for you and your boys

Whenever a problem exists, humans try to understand it. We make assumptions and analyze data in order to determine the cause of whatever issue is before us. It is our belief that if we understand the origin of a problem, we can then work out a solution. In most cases, this is true—the solution to a problem often comes from fully understanding its root causes.

The main problem with studying root causes, however, is in our DNA. Human brains are designed to think about problems in the simplest terms possible. Normally, that is good. Many times, the simplest answer is the best, most accurate one. Unfortunately, we are not always good at separating simple problems from complex ones. If there is a problem before us, we look for the simplest answer, no matter how complicated the issue is.

Simple problems require simple answers. Complicated problems require complicated solutions. Complicated solutions require *reflective thinking.*

The terms *reflective* thinking and *critical* thinking are often used interchangeably. But I like the term *reflective thinking* because it takes the aspects of critical thinking and adds an important step: reflecting on your beliefs and attitudes. Along with looking at a problem from multiple angles and trying to find information that disproves your working theory,[37] you must also consider *how* you think and feel about certain problems and *how* those thoughts and feelings might affect your judgment.[38] That type of reflective thinking helps us reduce our biases and come to more solid conclusions. And when we master reflective-thinking techniques, we end up teaching our boys how to do the same.

---

[37] aka *critical thinking*
[38] aka *reflective thinking*

It is the boys (and girls) who can think critically and reflectively to solve complicated problems who are going to change the world.

Skipping the reflective-thinking step in decision-making can have dire consequences

Here is a real-world example of the dangers of jumping to conclusions: In 2004, a researcher who was working on her dissertation discovered that anesthesiologists-in-training were susceptible to becoming fixated on one simple solution to a problem and ignoring important patient data in the process. This researcher found that these doctors would often fail to take into account all of the information they were receiving about a patient when that patient started showing signs of distress during an operation. The doctors would assume they knew the solution to the problem instead of questioning their assumptions and taking into consideration the full complexity of the situation. The author of this study concluded that the doctors' ability to successfully manage the crisis situation had nothing to do with their intelligence or technical knowledge—all of the doctors were smart and knew how to handle a plethora of medical emergencies. Instead, the doctors who failed to handle the crisis properly were those who had limited ability to reflect on their decisions, to communicate with others, and to analyze their own thinking process. They literally could not think about *how* they were thinking. The researcher went on to discover that reflection, communication, and thinking about the process of thinking is not natural. Instead, it takes great effort to do so. But, it can be done.[39]

> **TIP #001:** Train yourself to slow down your thinking process. **Reflect** on why you jump to the particular solution you jump to. What is

---

[39] Rudolph (2004)

it about that solution that makes sense to you? Why is that solution more appealing to you than others? How does your background influence your current decision-making? What other information might be helpful for you to understand before settling on your solution? What information exists that bolsters your argument? What information exists that disproves your theory? Who could you talk to (or correspond with) who might be able to provide you with more details regarding the situation in question?

You might ask yourself what this discussion has to do with raising boys. As we have established, boys—as they are currently being raised—are sometimes a problem,[40] with violence, anger, lack of communication, strife, and so on. And popular culture is rife with explanations as to why this problem exists. The explanations seem so simple: It's mental illness! It's video games! It's guns!

But as we have learned, the explanations are likely not that straightforward. We use our own cognitive shortcuts. Just like the smart, well-trained, ineffective anesthesiologists[41] who jumped to conclusions, we have the capacity to rush to answer the question, find blame, and feel better because we have diagnosed the problem. We then implement a solution. And then it doesn't work.

That is what reflective thinking has to do with raising boys. If we are able to reflect on our preconceived ideas as to why society has a problem, we can then develop some meaningful solutions.

---

[40] With the following caveat: most of the time, boys are not a problem. Don't panic! You are probably not raising a sociopath. But you might be able to do a little better...the idea is to go from good to great.

[41] Keep in mind, these are doctors whose sole job is to put you into a coma and bring you back alive. Do you really want them taking shortcuts and assuming *anything*?

TIP #002: Hold others accountable for their explanations. Whether they are friends, family members, news agencies, talking heads, radio personalities, or strangers on a bus, think about their explanations and solutions to problems with the same level of *reflection* that you give to your own thoughts on the subject at hand.

Reflecting on common explanations for the problems facing boys and men

In the spirit of avoiding the problem of oversimplifying problems and developing ineffective solutions, it seems important to reflect on some issues that frequently get blamed for causing aggression, violence, and mayhem in boys. The following are some commonly suggested negative influences on boys:

1. Violent Video Games and Movies

2. Easy Access To Guns

3. The Breakdown of the "Traditional Family"

4. The Lack of Religion in Everyday Life

5. Biology: Testosterone Causes Boys To Be Aggressive

6. How Boys Are Raised To Be Aggressive, Angry, and Competitive

7. It's Only A Problem For Boys With Mental Illness

A quick Internet search will reveal hundreds of news articles, opinion pieces, and blog posts that claim one of these seven factors is the problem—the main reason for boys going bad. But is there any truth to these claims? In order to answer this question, we will examine each claim, one by one.

Violent video games and movies

Albert Bandura, one of the pioneers of behavioral psychology and social learning theory, developed a series of experiments in the early 1960s, in which he studied children's reactions after watching a grown up punch an inflatable doll that looked like Bobo The Clown.[42] He had children watch adults act aggressively toward the clown doll, and he then purposefully frustrated the kids by taking away a bunch of toys. As you might expect, he discovered that watching both live adults and filmed adults act aggressively toward the clown led the frustrated children to act out aggressively toward the doll. This happened more often with boys than girls. Interestingly, he also noted the increase of verbal aggression in the children who watched the live adult hit the clown doll. He took his studies several steps further and discovered that children were much more likely to act aggressively after watching cartoon violence, and their aggressive behavior did not lessen when they saw the adult get punished for punching the clown. In all cases, the frustrated boys were more aggressive than the frustrated girls.[43]

So, that seems to be the end of it. Violent movies and games cause aggression. Simple.

Except it's *not* that simple. Remember, reflecting on these problems can often uncover a fairly complicated explanation.

In this case, Bandura's study only looked at children from ages three through six. And adults purposely frustrated them—they tried to get these poor boys and girls angry *on purpose*. And although they were more aggressive right after watching someone act aggressively, that does not mean this potential for aggression lasts more than a few minutes.

---

[42] To me, the study would have been much more interesting if the adults had punched actual clowns.

[43] Bandura, et al. (1961), (1963), (1965)

TIP #003: Try not to expose your boys to aggression, especially when they are young. That includes adults behaving aggressively in front of them, along with allowing them to watch violent movies and cartoons or play violent video games. Although we don't yet know if it has any long-term effect on overall aggression in boys, avoiding violence can make your family's everyday life easier. Stop reading for a moment and imagine what your life would be like if you stopped accidentally setting your boys up for getting aggressive every time they are frustrated. No more violent movies, no more violent cartoons, no more violent video games. If that reduced the number of times your son smacked his sister when she steals a toy from him, or it reduced the amount of angry screaming when dinner isn't quite ready—wouldn't that be nice? It might be difficult to wean your boy off these violent games and shows, but you have been through worse. You survived toilet training. You should be able to survive your son being bitter for a while because he can no longer watch violence on the screen.

TIP #004: In fact, limiting all screen time for your boys is a good way to go. There is no need to cut it off completely, but make sure your boys are engaging with quality programming. And while you are at it, you should cut down on your own screen time as well. It doesn't do you any good to sit in front of the television for hours, and your boys will learn from you modeling positive behavior. Make it a family challenge—no one will use more than 30 minutes of electronics per day.

No television on Saturdays. Phones get turned off at 7:30. Whatever the challenge, make the whole family stick to it. After some initial pain, you will be much better off.

Research over the past several decades on television and video game violence has been inconclusive. Studies have shown an increase in aggression only for a few moments after watching violent media, just like the Bandura experiments. Other research has shown an increase in aggression over the long-term. Still more studies have shown no relationship between violent media and long-term aggression.

Clearly, more research is needed in this field before a definitive answer can be reached. But one recent study starts to point the way toward a reasonable answer. In it, several Canadian psychologists examined teenagers over a period of several years, and they discovered that increasing the amount of time teens played violent video games increased their aggression over that period. They looked at teens who were already aggressive *and* teens who were not aggressive at all, and it did not matter. More violent games led to more consistent aggression for everyone involved in the study.[44]

> **TIP #005:** Don't let your boys play too many violent video games. Young children should not be exposed to any type of violent games. Older children may be able to handle slightly increased levels of violence. But even high school-aged kids are young and impressionable. You increase their potential for violence if you allow them to play violent games, even if they aren't violent to begin with.

---

[44] Willoughby, et al. (2012)

Easy access to guns

There is no way to know exactly how many guns are in existence in the United States, but the FBI estimates it is likely somewhere between 200 and 300 million. That is almost one gun for every American man, woman, and child. A growing number of people argue that guns are to blame for aggression and violence in boys. If the guns weren't there, boys would not be so dangerous. After all, more Americans now die in gun violence than die in car crashes every year.[45] Children die accidentally from gunshots. Shooters bring guns to school. Husbands kill wives and then themselves. Isn't it possible that guns are the problem?

It is certainly possible, but the issue is not as simple as it seems. Certainly, one of the best predictors of whether someone will die during the course of an act of violence is whether a gun is used to perpetrate that violence. But do guns actually *make* boys violent? Let's reflect on that question.

Many boys first experience toy guns at a young age. In 1992, researchers from Brandeis University studied three to five-year-old children and the effect toy guns have on their level of aggression. They found a relationship between these children playing with toy guns and real aggressive behavior (as opposed to play or pretend aggression). The kids who played with toy guns were also the kids who were more aggressive.[46]

So, there you have it. Toy guns lead to aggression in boys. Except ... maybe not. In the study, these researchers found correlations between playing with a toy gun and aggression. That does not mean toy guns *cause* aggression. It could be that aggressive boys choose to play with toy guns as a way of working out their aggression.

---

[45] Data from the Centers For Disease Control and Prevention
[46] Watson, et al. (1992)

Or it could be that something else causes both toy gun play *and* aggressiveness. For example, these same researchers, in the *exact same study*, discovered a relationship between parental punishment and real aggressive behavior. The more extreme a parent's punishment, the more aggressive the boy will be. Maybe that causes a boy to seek outlets for his aggression, such as aggressive play with toy guns.

> **TIP #006:** There are ways for you to shape your boys' behavior and get them to act properly that do not involve harsh punishment. Of course, punishment is going to be necessary at times, but not always. And it is not always helpful. In fact, excessive punishment will likely do the exact opposite of what you would like it to do for your boys: It will make them worse, not better. Instead of a harsh punishment, try giving your son a five to fifteen-minute time-out in his room. Many times, he just needs to be "reset" rather than punished. It is possible that a short break is all he needs to readjust his behavior. By the way, this same technique works for adults. If you feel yourself start to spin out of control, give yourself a five-minute break—if possible. It really helps.

We have learned there is little evidence that toy guns increase a boy's level of aggression, but there *is* some relationship between the two. In looking further into the research, the picture starts to clear a bit more. For example, researchers from the United Kingdom discovered that when male college students held and interacted with guns for a period of time, their testosterone levels increased, as did their aggression toward others. By the time boys enter late adolescence, they understand the difference between real and toy guns—their testosterone and aggression levels only increased after handling a real gun.[47]

Other researchers have found similar results. One research team discovered that merely looking at pictures of guns increased aggressive thoughts in boys and men.[48] This same research team studied the phenomenon further and realized that both hunters and non-hunters had more aggressive thoughts after looking at pictures of guns—indicating that gun safety and familiarity around guns does not necessarily cause a decrease in the level of aggression experienced in boys.[49]

Essentially, it has been known for decades that the presence of a gun increases aggression in the moment. It even has a name—it is called *the weapons effect*.[50]

Case closed—guns are bad. Except ... that is not always the case. Researchers from the Netherlands studied the differences in aggression between members of shooting associations versus nonmembers. These individuals' personalities were studied separately from the presence of guns (in other words, they hadn't just seen or shot a gun). The researchers found that members of shooting associations tended to be less aggressive, impulsive, and neurotic than nonmembers.[51] Other researchers discovered that the decision for adolescent boys to actually carry a gun revolved around those boys' need for acceptance from their peer group and their level of aggression.[52] It wasn't necessarily that the guns caused the aggression in boys. It was actually the other way around—the boys who were more aggressive chose to carry guns. It didn't hurt that these same boys often had friends who also carried guns.

---

[47] Klinesmith, et al. (2006).
[48] Anderson, et al. (1998)
[49] Bartholow, et al. (2005)
[50] Berkowitz & LePage (1967)
[51] Nagtegaal (2009)
[52] Dijkstra, et al. (2010)

So guns might be bad, but they might not be. F.
research, it appears that boys who are trying to feel powerful w
be more prone to want to carry a gun. But boys who grow up with
a familiarity around guns may or may not be more aggressive
than others.

With all of this in mind, it is extremely important to note that
gun-safety training works. For all boys. Of all ages.[53] Training
tends to work best for boys who engage in hands-on safety
classes. However, merely discussing gun safety without guns
present is helpful. Even radio public service announcements lead
to an increase in gun safety.[54] An important caveat to mention is
that gun-safety training is less effective for younger boys than it
is for older boys.[55] It still helps, but younger boys (up to six years
old) tend to have a hard time resisting playing with a gun if it
is around.

Based on a reflective review of the research, a few main
trends emerge:

1. Aggressive boys tend to be drawn to guns, no matter
   their age.

2. Guns increase aggression in boys who are not familiar
   with them.

3. Younger boys (up to age five or six) are at fairly high risk of
   playing with guns if they are available. No amount of gun-
   safety training will completely eliminate this.

4. Gun-safety training works incredibly well for boys starting
   around age six or seven.

5. Familiarity with guns and shooting may actually decrease
   aggression and the dangerous *weapons effect*.

---

[53] Himle, et al. (2004); Miltenberger, et al. (2005)
[54] Meyer, et al. (2003)
[55] Hardy, et al. (1996)

TIP #007: If you do not want your boys to be raised around guns, do not allow them to have access to them. Even toy guns will increase their level of aggression. There are hundreds of other toys for your boys to enjoy.

TIP #008: If you want your boys to be raised around guns, do not allow them to have access to guns without supervision, and take the time to teach your boys how to interact appropriately and safely with guns. Teach them yourself, and also sign them up for gun-safety classes. If you do these things, your boys will most likely be safe, and grow into responsible adults. They may even be less aggressive because of their appropriate gun use.

The breakdown of the "Traditional Family"

The traditional family is a husband, a wife, and 2.5 children. The *breakdown of the traditional family* is usually code for one of two scenarios—single moms or gay couples. We have all heard the arguments: Raising a child out of wedlock causes all kinds of societal problems, including poverty, crime, and aggression. Gay couples raising children cannot teach them the valuable skills that come from having opposite sex parents. If there is no male in the home, or no traditional male, how can boys learn to become responsible, powerful men?

We will examine all of these issues in this section, but first, here is a common sense tip: Even if the breakdown of the traditional family does cause societal problems, that is not an excuse if the boys who grow up in *your* house become unproductive members of society. In fact, if you express hostile, judgmental views toward *nontraditional families* around your children, they will pick up on that hostility, and will quickly recognize that other people, even those with like-minded *but non-hostile* views, find you fairly repulsive.[56]

> **TIP #009:** Take responsibility for your parenting. If your boys end up turning into jerks, that is your fault—not the fault of your gay neighbors or the single mom down the street. In fact, your judgment of those nontraditional families may be turning your boys into worse people.

Some individuals point to single mothers as a major part of the problem. The logic is that it is difficult for any one person to raise a child, let alone a woman who might have difficulty understanding how to properly socialize a boy. There have been numerous studies over the years that indicate this may be the case. But researchers from New York have recently discovered otherwise. Children raised by single mothers do not act out at a rate higher than children raised by two parents. In fact, when the researchers parsed the data, they found a surprising result: Girls raised by single mothers tend to have more difficulty in life than girls raised by two parents. But boys raised by single mothers do *not* differ from boys raised by two parents.[57] So single mothers do not seem to raise bad boys any more often than two parent families do.

> **TIP #010:** If you are a single mother and experiencing judgmental attitudes about your ability to raise a boy, tell those judgmental do-gooders to stuff a sock in it. You probably aren't going to do any worse than they are.

In the spirit of reflective thought, it seems important to also examine whether single mothers can instill masculine values in boys the same way two-parent households can. The quick answer is a definitive *yes*. In studies from 1997 and 2004, boys who lacked

[56] Mae (2001)
[57] Mokrue, et al. (2012)

a father in their lives revealed they tend to have different relationships with their mothers than boys with fathers do, but there are
no negative consequences to the boys' healthy development. In
fact, they grow up to be just as masculine as boys with a mother
and a father. They do, however, also display more feminine traits,
which may help them to be more well-rounded individuals.[58]

> **TIP #011:** Many parenting experts will tell single
> mothers to find men in their lives who can help
> their sons develop masculine traits. This advice
> is misguided, though. Regardless of whether a
> son grows up with a father in the home, he will
> develop masculine traits.

Furthermore, the studies that claimed "fatherless" boys have
significant problems in their lives are from the 1960s and 1970s.
Newer research shows these problems have mostly disappeared.
In fact, most boys raised by single mothers who have behavioral
problems and grow up to be unproductive members of society live
in families with multiple risk factors: mental illness, poverty, hostility in the home, substance abuse, physical or sexual assaults,
and so on. Boys in two-parent homes with the same risk factors
fare just as poorly.[59] When these risk factors are removed, boys
from single-parent and two-parent homes fare equally well.

> **TIP #012:** Regardless of the number of parents
> in the household, take stock of the risk factors
> that could cause your boys to develop life-
> long problems:
>
> 1. Untreated mental illness in one or more of
>   the parents
>
> 2. Overt hostility in the home

[58] MacCallum, et al. (1997); MacCallum Golombok
(2004)
[59] Florsheim, et al. (1998)

3. Overly harsh discipline

4. Substance abuse

5. Domestic violence and/or child physical or sexual abuse

6. Poverty

If any of these risk factors is present, you need to think about how best to address the problem. In many cases, psychotherapy and medication may be necessary. In some extreme cases, the authorities need to be alerted.

Upon reflection, the latest psychological research suggests that single mothers are not a major problem for boys, unless there are also a number of other risk factors in the home. But what about boys raised by a gay or lesbian couple? The same studies cited above, from 1997 and 2004, also apply to lesbian couples, as they were included in those studies. A review of the research shows that boys who are adopted by two men fare just as well and have a similar set of potential problems as boys adopted by heterosexual couples.[60] And the overwhelming scientific evidence is that boys raised by gay couples are at equal risk for developing lifelong emotional problems as boys raised by heterosexual parents.[61]

To sum up, a reflective examination of nontraditional families does not explain why boys sometimes go bad.

The lack of religion in everyday life

Many people argue that the decreasing importance of religion in many Americans' lives can lead boys to develop emotional and behavioral problems. This reasoning makes sense. Religion

---

[60] Farr & Patterson (2013)
[61] Golombok & Tasker (1994)

instills a sense of morals and a set of pro-social rules we all must follow. If these rules get thrown to the wayside, it may be that boys will not know how to behave.

Certainly, religion can have an immensely positive impact on a boy's life. Without getting into the theological arguments for religion, there are real psychological benefits. For example, boys who are exposed to religion and who use religious coping mechanisms, such as praying and relying on faith to get through difficult times, have higher achievement motivation than boys who do not use those religious coping mechanisms. These boys are also more resilient in the face of violence—boys who are religious and exposed to acts of violence will react better than those who are not religious.

Boys who are exposed to religion also tend to experience their lives as having more meaning, which has been shown to be a protective factor against stress, depression, and violence.[62] Further, adolescent boys tend to have higher life satisfaction when they engage in some sort of daily spiritual experience, when they participate in a forgiving society, and when they experience the support of their community. Interestingly, frequency of attending religious services does not predict life satisfaction, but the feeling of community and daily spiritual experience does.[63]

There are hundreds of other studies demonstrating the positive benefits of religion in boys' lives. Their results can be boiled down to a common set of factors. If you answer yes to the following questions, religion can be very good for your boys:

1. Is your religious community open and supportive of all boys? *Seriously—all boys, whether straight or gay, tall or short, fat or skinny, racial or ethnic majority or minority.*

2. Does your community actively encourage forgiveness for wrongdoing?

---

[62] LeBlanc (2008)
[63] Kim, et al. (2012)

3. Are there daily religious or spiritual activities (no matter how large or small) in which your boys can engage?

4. Does your community support fostering a sense of meaning in boys' lives?

5. Does your religious tradition encourage using religiously based coping mechanisms to deal with life's difficulties?

> **TIP #013:** Answer the above questions, one through five, honestly. If you answered 'yes' to three or more of the questions, chances are your boys' religious upbringing will have a positive impact on their lives. If you answered 'no' to three or four questions, your religious beliefs may not be helping your boys, and in fact, may be harming them. You may need to think critically about why your religious community is lacking in these fundamental areas.

Although the presence of religion and supportive religious communities can have a positive impact on boys' lives, that does not necessarily mean that the absence of religion has a negative impact. The *lack of religion in a boy's life* has not been directly explored in a scientific manner. But logic would dictate that boys who are raised with a lack of religion in the home may not be exposed to the positive benefits and coping mechanisms that religion can provide.

> **TIP #014:** If you are raising your boys in a non-religious environment, you will need to consider the idea that your boys may be missing out on a number of potential religiously based benefits.

And it gets more complicated when examining religious traditions that are fundamentalist and highly rigid in their worldview. An Oklahoma researcher examined this issue and discovered that helping boys develop their faith does not increase anger or prejudice toward others. However, the same researcher discovered that teaching religious fundamentalism and authoritarianism *did* increase boys' hatred and prejudice toward others.[64] Another researcher, from California, found that religious fundamentalism limited boys' ability to think critically and reflect fully on the problems they later faced in life.[65] One more researcher, this one from Texas, discovered that college-aged boys who grew up in a fundamentalist home had poor intellectual and moral development compared to their non-fundamentalist peers.[66] They had more trouble determining the most ethical course of action when faced with a moral dilemma.

> **TIP #015:** Should you raise your boys in a religious household, or is it bad for their development? This is not a theological book, and giving advice about a family's spirituality is not the goal of this chapter. But what evidence exists points to the fact that, although religion can be psychologically good for boys, fundamentalism has some definite bad psychological consequences for them. It hinders their ability to think, and they are less equipped to reflect and reason their way through moral problems. A good goal is to examine your family's religious beliefs and practices to determine if they allow room for questioning, reflective thought, and inclusiveness. If they don't, there is a good chance you will raise boys who struggle in these areas and who will not be able to make good ethical decisions. If your goal is to raise a mighty, spiritual boy, you

---

[64] Crownover (2011)
[65] Garo (2006)
[66] Copeland (1995)

must give him the tools to think through vexing problems in a serious manner.

Biology: testosterone causes boys' aggression

Boys are different from girls. They have more testosterone. That causes them to be more aggressive, angrier, more competitive, and more prone to behavioral problems. There is nothing that can be done about it. Boys are just more aggressive than girls.

Intuitively, that sentiment makes sense. In almost every species on earth, the males are larger than the females. They are more muscular and they are more aggressive. They fight. They jockey for position among other males. They stake out their territory. They pee on trees.[67]

Humans are animals too. There is nothing we can do to change our biology. Right?

But consider what else the males of other species do in the course of a normal life: They fight; they kill; they rape; they impregnate females and leave them to raise the babies. They are mostly loners who seek out companionship only when they have the biological urge for sex.

This is not an accurate description of the average human man. There are men who engage in some or all of the aforementioned activities, but they are considered abnormal—psychopaths who are beyond help. The average man does not act like a complete animal.[68]

So what is the difference between men and other animals? Our brains. Humans have the same primitive brain structures as every other mammal—structures that help us breathe, sleep, react to danger, learn, and remember information. But we also have something extra: portions of the brain called the frontal lobe and

---

[67] This really happens.
[68] He will pee on trees occasionally, though.

the prefrontal cortex. Other mammals have these too, but ours are a lot better developed. These are the portions of our brain that allow us to (among other things) think reflectively, control our impulses, and regulate our emotions.

Where other animals experience only primitive emotions— such as fear, excitement, and anger—humans are able to recognize and experience a wide range of emotional experiences. Sad, happy, angry, frustrated, depressed, anxious, stressed, calm, excited, elated, verklempt, tearful, melancholy, reticent, skeptical, cautiously optimistic ... these are just a few of the emotions we are able to experience, based on a combination of our natural urges and our ability to think in a complicated manner about what is going on around us.

With all that in mind, men are not ruled by testosterone any more than *any* human is ruled by any chemical or hormone released in his or her body. Those chemicals help shape a particular behavior or emotional experience, but humans are typically in complete control of their emotions and their behavior. If they choose to be in control, that is.

> **TIP #016:** Don't let anyone tell you that boys
> will be boys because of the testosterone pumping
> through their systems. If they are acting badly,
> that is almost always something you can fix.

In the spirit of using the portions of our brains that are better developed than wolves (for example), we should reflect a little deeper on the issue of testosterone and its effect on boys and men.

The simplest explanation is that, yes, testosterone does have an effect. But the effect could be good *or* bad, depending on a lot of other factors.

For example, researchers from the Netherlands wanted to learn whether higher levels of testosterone for boys *in utero* led to psychopathic behavior later in life. What they discovered is fascinating: There is a definite relationship between testosterone and bad behaviors later in life. The higher the fetal testosterone levels, the higher the chances of a boy becoming a psychopath. Except ... this finding only held true when there were also other environmental risk factors present in the boys' lives after their birth—factors such as social rejection and poverty (along with a few genetic risk factors). When these environmental risk factors were not present in the boys' lives, high fetal testosterone levels predicted high levels of motivation, assertiveness, fairness, and leadership ability.[69] All of a sudden, testosterone doesn't sound so bad.

Unfortunately, it is not quite that simple. Temporarily increased levels of testosterone in boys can cause anger,[70] and high prenatal testosterone levels can cause vulnerable boys—those with the environmental risk factors already mentioned—to have relatively uncontrollable behavioral problems.[71] High testosterone levels can also lead to higher suicide rates among men with mental illness.[72] Finally, increased levels of testosterone can lead to significantly higher sex drive for boys and men.[73] [74]

Essentially, testosterone can be a problem for boys, but only if there are other warning signs present. It can cause anger, aggression, suicidal thinking, psychopathic behaviors, and problems with acting out. But it can be a highly positive influence in boys' lives if those warning signs aren't present. It can cause high levels of motivation, achievement, leadership, and a heightened sense of fairness. In the heat of the moment, your boys' testosterone levels may spike, causing some temporary frustration or anger,

---

[69] Yildirim & Derksen (2012)

[70] Peterson & Harmon-Jones (2012)

[71] Liu, et al. (2012)

[72] Sher (2012); Sher, et al. (2012)

[73] As shown in, like, virtually every study ever done on testosterone and sex drive in the last 60 years.

[74] There is not necessarily anything wrong with a strong sex drive, unless it is coupled with impulsivity and aggression, which can become problematic.

but remember, we humans have good frontal lobes and excellent prefrontal cortices. Your son can learn to control his impulses and regulate his emotions during these testosterone spikes.

> **TIP #017:** Run a quick check on your boys to determine if they were exposed to higher than normal levels of testosterone in utero. Compare the length of your boys' second fingers (index fingers) to their fourth fingers (ring fingers). Measure the length of both fingers, from the crease to the tip of the finger. Then divide the length of the index finger by the length of the ring finger. You will then get a ratio, referred to as the 2D:4D ratio. Lower ratios indicate a higher level of prenatal testosterone exposure. Normally, the second finger is longer than the fourth finger.

> **TIP #018:** If you think your boys were exposed to a lot of testosterone in utero, don't automatically assume you are raising future sociopaths. Instead, look through the following list of risk factors. The more questions you answer in the affirmative, the higher the chances your boys may develop problematic behaviors (especially when combined with high fetal testosterone exposure):
>
> 1. Is your boy being raised around someone who is overly angry or hostile?
>
> 2. Is your boy being raised in poverty or in an area of low-socioeconomic status?
>
> 3. Has your boy experienced rejection by his peers at school/preschool?

4. Does your boy display acting out or problematic behavior?

5. Does your boy have trouble focusing or paying attention at an age-appropriate level?

6. Does your boy have male relatives who have displayed significant antisocial behavior, such as breaking the law, spending time in jail, fighting, or exhibiting a lack of empathy toward others (note: these should be relatives your boy is related to by blood)?

NOTE: This is a general rule of thumb, and there are exceptions to every rule. You know your boy best, and if you answered 'yes' to many of the above questions, it is not an absolute guarantee of problems later in life.

TIP #019: If you have calculated the 2D:4D ratio for your boys and discovered that they have been exposed to higher than normal levels of fetal testosterone, and you answered 'no' to all or most of the questions from **TIP #018**, the research is on your side. It is possible that your boys are being raised in an enriching environment with no genetic predispositions toward psychopathy. They have the potential to be leaders who value achievement, motivation, and fairness in their lives.

Here's one last note on testosterone and our brains: If you think boys who are only aggressive, impulsive, physically strong, or highly active are *all boy*, you are very much mistaken. In fact, they are missing a major component of what it means to be a boy, or a human for that matter—they are missing the use of their frontal lobes. They are, literally, not *all boy* because they are choosing to turn off an important part of their brains.

On the contrary, boys who express emotion, remain stable, stay in control, lead others, and assert their opinions properly are truly *all boy*. They are using their natural testosterone levels and tempering their behavior with their frontal lobes.

How boys are socialized: aggression, competition, anger

One last commonly cited reason for aggression, anger, and other behavioral problems in boys is how they are socialized. Information from the testosterone section of this chapter would argue that this may be the case—after all, testosterone can be either a positive or a negative in a boy's life, depending on the circumstances under which he is raised. But it is important to dive deeper into information on the socialization of emotion and behavior in boys.

As far as emotions are concerned, numerous studies confirm that boys and girls are socialized differently and that mothers and fathers socialize their children in different ways. For example, mothers are more involved with discouraging anger in both genders than are fathers. And fathers reward girls for expressing emotions like sadness and fear, but they punish boys for express-ing those same emotions.[75] Both fathers and mothers tend to punish older adolescents more than younger children for displays of emotion. Parents also punish kids more for emotional displays when those kids have behavioral problems.[76] With aggression,

---

[75] Garside, et al. (2002)
[76] Klimes-Dougan, et al. (2007)

there is support for the notion that preschool boys and girls both react equally aggressively toward their peers as a way of solving problems. Girls are then quickly taught to demure to others rather than remain aggressive or assertive. Boys do not appear to go through this same socialization process. Thus, in this case, it seems that a *lack* of socialization might be to blame for boys' aggression—parents and teachers may fail to act in a manner that would discourage aggression in preschool-aged boys.[77] It is the *boys will be boys* phenomenon in practice.

Further study has demonstrated that boys around the age of ten have been socialized to express their aggression directly and expressively, whereas girls have been taught to express their aggression in more indirect, passive ways. Interestingly, both boys and girls of this age experience about the same amount of aggression—they have just learned to express it differently.[78] In fact, girls who have been socialized in a similar manner to boys demonstrate just as much overt physical aggression as boys.[79]

Based on a reflective examination of the research, socialization is sometimes related to the negative emotional reactions that boys exhibit, along with behavioral problems such as aggressiveness. In the vast majority of studies reviewed, boys and girls initially have the same propensity toward a vast array of emotional expression, and are equally physically aggressive, but our socialization of boys and girls differs. Boys quickly learn to suppress emotions other than anger, and they are *not* discouraged to quell their overt aggression.

One research article pointing out the differences between boys and girls suggested that we should socialize our boys to be like girls. Seriously.

Here is a better suggestion: Reward your boys for expressing *any* emotion they experience. Anger—reward it. Sadness—reward

---

[77] Hay, et al. (2011)
[78] Brodzinsky, et al. (1979)
[79] Eron (1980)

it. Happiness—reward it. Fear—reward it. Boys should be encouraged to express all of their emotions and to fully experience them; if they don't, the emotions will get bottled up and eventually come out in negative ways.

There is a catch though. It is important to reward the expression of the emotion, but *discourage* the acting-out behavior. Tell your boy it is okay for him to be angry—everyone gets angry sometimes—but let him know, in no uncertain terms, that temper tantrums, throwing objects, and hitting people is not acceptable. Teach him that he can (and should) feel his aggressive emotions, without acting on them. The same goes for sadness or fear—it is okay to be sad and it is okay to be scared, and it is okay to cry—but uncontrollable tears and panic attacks are not acceptable.

> **TIP #020:** Help your boys regain control of their emotions. Don't discourage them from feeling, but let them know that acting out emotionally is not appropriate. "It is okay for you to be sad now," you can say. "That happens to everyone. It is even okay to cry. But you are out of control, and that is not okay. Let me help you get back into control." Or you can say, "You need to go to your room until you can get yourself back under control. It is not okay to act out of control like that around other people." (Special note: Crying in public is not out of control. Blubbering, flopping around on the ground, and expelling liquid from several facial orifices at once is out of control.)

Here are five techniques you can use to encourage emotional expression in your boys, while at the same time discouraging emotional acting out:

1. Five deep breaths: Have them count to five as they are breathing in and count to five again as they are breathing

out. Repeat this pattern for a total of five breaths. Breathe deeply with them. It sounds simple, but this really works, especially if you have your boys practice it a few times when they are not feeling overly emotional.

2. A good bear hug: Being touched and squeezed can have a soothing effect. It can also feel confining if done in a punitive manner. Make it clear to them that you are not trying to pin them down, you are trying to give them a calming bear hug. Explain this process and practice it prior to an emotional outburst. And if a particular boy starts reacting badly to this technique, immediately let go and try something else. You will just make it worse by hanging on like you are riding a bucking bronco. That panicking boy will think he is being punished for showing emotion.

3. The Rocking Power Grip: This is an offshoot of the bear hug. Have him sit with his knees bent. Then have him wrap his arms around his shins and hug them as tightly as he can to his chest. Then have him gently rock back and forth. This position and motion can have an incredibly soothing effect, especially if practiced a few times when calm.

4. If all else fails, isolate: Explain to your boys that they are out of control, and that you have tried but can not help them to calm down, so they need to go to their room until they can calm *themselves*. Explain that they are not getting in trouble or receiving a time out—they just need to figure out how to calm themselves down because their behavior is not appropriate for public.

5. If all else *really* fails, get professional help: There are certain mental health issues—like depression, anxiety, and impulse-control disorders—that can cause out-of-control

emotions and behavior. These issues need to be treated by professionals.

Mental illness is the problem

This section can be short, with very little reflection necessary. Aggression and violence is not just a problem for boys with mental illness. It is a potential problem for every boy. The research on this is very clear: People with mental illness are no more violent than people without mental illness. There is too much data to cite one or two research articles on this matter. It's just the plain truth: Mental illness on its own is not a good predictor of violence.

One caveat to the above statement is that children who are depressed have a somewhat higher likelihood of displaying aggressive behaviors than non-depressed children. In a study of third, fourth, and fifth graders in Tennessee, researchers found a link between depression and aggressive behavior.[80]

According to the American Psychiatric Association,[81] the common symptoms of depression are as follows:

1. Sadness most of the day, every day, for a period of at least two weeks

2. Excessive anger

3. A lack of interest in activities he used to enjoy

4. Appetite or sleep changes

5. Low energy and fatigue

6. Feelings of worthlessness or guilt

7. Problems with concentration and thinking

---

80 Panak & Garber (1992)
81 APA (2013)

8. Thoughts of death and/or suicidal thinking

> **TIP #021:** Be mindful of depressive traits in your boys. If they are experiencing depression, they are more likely to be aggressive and have conduct problems at home and at school.

Likewise, when boys have parents who are depressed and hostile, they are much more likely to become aggressive.[82]

> **TIP #022:** If you want to raise your boys to be productive and happy, don't expose them to your own hostility. If you are an angry person, you will raise an angry boy. Figure out a way to snap out of it. Deal with your anger, get therapy, take medications, do whatever. But if you are hostile, your boys will have a much harder time behaving responsibly in the world.

One more caveat about mental illness and aggression: Most major acts of violence in the world are caused by individuals with mental illness. But most individuals with mental illness are no more dangerous than the average person.

To put the above statement into context, most major acts of violence in the world are also caused by gun owners. But gun ownership by itself is a lousy predictor of future violence. Most gun owners are peaceful, caring people. The same is true of individuals with mental illness.

Summary

We have learned some interesting facts about boys in this chapter. We have dispelled a few myths, and we have confirmed some widely held views on boys' development. And along the way, we may have gotten angry and anxious.

---

[82] Knox, et al. (2011)

Critical, reflective thinking is an important skill in any endeavor. And this chapter is a demonstration of how powerful it can be. Complicated problems rarely have simple causes or solutions, no matter how hard we try to believe otherwise. By forcing ourselves to fully reflect on problems and potential solutions, we will be able to develop effective solutions—small pieces of a puzzle that can have a huge impact.

This type of thinking is not always fun. It is hard to be told we are wrong. It is painful to think about the flaws in our deeply held beliefs.

The results of reflective thinking are not always popular either. After all, we have discovered in this chapter that guns are not always bad. In some cases, proper training and exposure to firearms actually reduces a boy's level of aggression. We have also discovered that fundamentalist religious thought, regardless of the denomination, can be bad for boys. These are not always easy truths to reconcile, but they are true nonetheless.

Not popular, not fun, but necessary. If you want to raise a boy who improves the world—a boy who is truly *all boy*—you must be willing to reflect on your deepest held thoughts on parenting and be willing to change yourself in some foundational ways.

> **TIP #023:** Be willing to question yourself and all of your beliefs. Not just the easy, surface-level beliefs. *All of them*. You likely won't need to change everything you believe, but you will probably need to change some of it. Be willing to do it. In the end, it will be worth it to your boys.

And don't panic. You're probably doing a fine job of raising your boys. We can all improve, though.

> **TIP #024:** Don't panic. The idea is not to be perfect. It is to take what you are already doing well and make it more effective. Along the way,

you can also drop some potentially bad parenting habits. We all have them.

CHAPTER 2.5

Words Matter: the differences between sympathy, compassion, and empathy

In upcoming chapters, I discuss the importance of empathy. In fact, the entire book is basically an explanation of the importance of instilling empathy in your boys.

Many people use the words *sympathy, compassion,* and *empathy* interchangeably, but they are most definitely different concepts. Thinking of them as the same can have some unintended negative consequences.

Let me briefly define the three concepts:

Sympathy is sharing a feeling with someone.

Compassion is feeling sorry for someone's misfortune.

Empathy is intellectually understanding why a person feels the way he/she is feeling.

On the surface, all three words sound like they mean the same thing, but they do not. It is possible for a person to have empathy for another person but feel no sympathy toward the individual. It is equally possible for a person to show another individual compassion without having an ounce of empathy. Of course, all three concepts are related, and a person who is more empathic is likely to be more compassionate.[83] But, it is not right to lump them all together as if they are the same concept.

For example, there is no reason why a person needs to share another's feelings, especially feelings of sadness or anger, in order to have empathy. After a thorough understanding of a murderer's life circumstances, a judge might be able to understand *why* the murderer was angry and *why* he felt he needed to kill his victim. But the judge does not need to *share* those feelings with the murderer. The judge may not even need to *feel* compassion toward the murderer. But the judge will be more likely to make an informed decision about the murderer's sentence by *having* empathy. Empathy is not a free pass. It is a tool we can use to get along with others. However, when we conflate empathy with compassion and sympathy, it can actually cloud our judgment and cause us to make decisions that do not benefit society as a whole.[84]

So for the rest of this book, think of empathy as an intellectual exercise and as something a person can *have* for one another. Sympathy and compassion are feeling states, and they are something a person can *feel* for one another.

Developing empathy does not mean turning into a pushover. In fact, it can lead to great strength in conflictual and moral situations, as understanding where another person is coming from is crucial. But that does not mean the empathizer needs to feel sorry for others or feel sympathy when no sympathy is due. This book is not about pitying others. It is about teaching boys to regulate their emotions and to have empathy toward others in order to grow into strong leaders and productive, honorable men.

---

[83] Johnson, et al. (2002)
[84] Breithaupt (2012); Choe & Min (2011)

CHAPTER 3

The One Rule: emotional expression and empathy improve just about everything

Socialization is the key: teach your boy to be a girl?
Remember the research article from Chapter 2 that offered the supremely helpful tip, 'Socialize Your Boy Like a Girl'? Well, that is what the next several chapters are about.

Sort of, although not really ... expressing emotions, learning to tone down aggression, empathizing with others—these are not girly traits, although girls benefit greatly from them. Rather they are traits that will allow your boys to be fully human and *all boy.* Here's a quick recap: We learned through extensive reflection from the last chapter that the way we socialize our children has a huge impact on how they develop—their emotional reactions, their aggressive tendencies, and their overall behavior. As parents and educators, it is our job to train our children to control their impulses and to treat others with respect. We need to teach them what behavior is okay and what behavior is not acceptable under any circumstances. We need to model to them the importance of thinking through situations fully and treating others in a fair and caring manner.

We also learned from Chapter 2 that boys and girls start out with the same potential for negative behavior—temper tantrums, aggression, and out-of-control behavior, just to name a few. We socialize girls differently than boys and we accidentally encourage our boys to squelch their emotions and express only anger when confronted with difficult situations. Girls who are socialized *to be like boys* do the same thing. And when you add testosterone to poor socialization, you create the potential for a big problem.

That is the bad news. If we continue doing what we have all been doing, some boys will suffer. But there is good news too. Most parents raise boys who are relatively normal. They don't start wars. They don't go on killing sprees, and they don't routinely get into barroom brawls. You are probably one of those parents who is going to raise a relatively normal boy, so cut yourself some slack.[85]

> **TIP #025:** Cut yourself some slack. No one is ever going to be the perfect parent. You just need to be the good-enough parent. And you're probably already good enough. See Tip #001 for more clarification.

There is more good news: There are changes you can make to your parenting that can have a dramatic effect on your boys. No matter their age, it is never too late to make positive changes. As they get older, the changes are harder, but change is still possible.

> **TIP #026:** Take comfort—it is not too late to make changes in your boys' lives. You can start doing things differently now that will help your boys improve their lives and eventually improve the world.

---

[85] The fact that you are reading this book is a good sign. You are obviously interested in parenting and want to raise good boys. As a result, your boy is probably not going to turn into a psychopath.

TIP #027: Don't go overboard. If you are stressed, worried about your boys' development, and fearful that nothing will work, you will not succeed. Try to relax a bit. There are a lot of tips in this book. You don't have to implement all of them at once. Pick out the parts that make the most sense to you and start there. Make a few small changes and see what happens. Then try out some other tips. There is no 'system' to this book—you do not need to start at TIP #001 and work your way forward systematically. And it will be impossible to follow all of the tips outlined in the book. Just pick the ones that make sense and that work for you and your boys. Go with those.

The benefits of teaching your boys to express emotion and have empathy

Your goal does not need be to teach your boys to be girls. But it is possible to change the way you shape their behavior in order to emphasize qualities that were once regarded as only appropriate for women. Essentially, you need to teach your boys to recognize and regulate their emotions, and understand other people's emotions.

That's it: recognize emotion, regulate emotion, and understand other people. That does not sound too girlie, does it?

It does sound overly simple, though. And if we've learned one thing from previous chapters, it is that most problems are not as simple as they seem. In this case, the solution sounds simple, but executing it is complicated. And before we get to the execution phase, let's cover the benefits of teaching your boys to be more in touch with their own emotions, and the emotions of others. By fully reflecting on the topic at hand, it will become easier to understand why such a simple solution can have such a dramatic effect.

Essentially, the benefits of socializing your boys to recognize, regulate, and understand emotion are as follows:

1. It will improve their behavior at home and at school;

2. They will be happier, more confident, and have more appropriate friends;

3. It will improve their conflict resolution skills;

4. They will do better in school and have a better chance of getting into college and/or finding a job;

5. It will help them, and you, identify true mental health problems more quickly (if any exist).

Improved behavior at home and school

As early as preschool, boys who are able to understand emotions and relate to others are more competent in school. A study from George Mason University and Virginia State University looked at preschool boys *and* girls, and they discovered that both genders were more ready to perform well in school if they had knowledge of emotions—in other words, they did better at school if they could recognize different emotions in themselves and others. These emotionally knowledgeable students also related better to their teachers and received higher teacher ratings.[86]

In older students, more emotional knowledge (understanding both their own emotions and the emotions of others) leads boys to bully less. Their peers view them in a more positive light. There is even some evidence that these students perform better academically.[87]

---

[86] Garner & Waajid (2008)
[87] Mavroveli & Sánchez-Ruiz (2011)

An interesting study from 2001 determined that boys have more problems when they have less emotional knowledge. The researchers had boys and their parents look at a series of pictures that would typically evoke either positive emotions, such as happiness, or negative emotions, such as sadness. They discovered that the boys who were less emotionally expressive in relation to the negative-emotion pictures were the ones who had the most behavior problems at home and school.[88]

As far as empathy goes, researchers from all over the world agree that increasing empathy in boys, or their understanding of the emotional states of others, leads to a decrease in aggression and behavioral problems. They also agree that empathy is not one of those traits you either have or you don't have—*it can be taught and learned*. The United States, Singapore, China, Italy, Iran ... it doesn't matter where the study was done, the conclusions were the same. It also didn't matter how old the boys studied were. Preschoolers as young as three years old were studied. Children in middle schools were studied, and so were high school students. Boys can learn empathy, and it improves their behavior. It decreases physical aggression. It decreases verbal aggression. It decreases bullying. It decreases cyber bullying. It decreases passive aggressiveness. It really works.[89]

> **TIP #028:** Teach your boys to recognize the emotions of others. It will improve their behavior at home and at school.

---

[88] Eisenberg, et al. (2001)
[89] Ang Goh (2010); Belacchi & Farina (2012); Jagers, et al. (2007); Vaziri & Afsaneh (2012); Wang, et al. (2012); Yeo, et al. (2011)

More happiness, more confidence, more (appropriate) friends

The International Journal of Behavioral Development published an ambitious study in 2011, examining over 1600 kids in grades six through eight. The researchers looked at all kinds of problematic behaviors and the factors that led to them. One of their important discoveries was that the influence of peers magnifies as boys grow older. If your boys are spending time with friends who are good, they will behave better. However, if they are hanging out with the wrong crowd, their behavior will deteriorate. The effects are dramatic in both the positive and negative direction.[90]

And, as you might expect, boys who are more empathic have better friends. A researcher from the University of Texas at Arlington discovered that boys who have more ability to recognize and understand the emotions of others tend to have higher quality friendships, and are less likely to be victimized by their friendships.[91]

Here is a list of suggestions you can use to help determine if your boys are spending time with the *right* friends:

1. Spend time getting to know the kids your boys are spending time with.

2. Meet the parents of your boys' friends. If the parents are jerks, the boys probably are too.

3. For younger boys, set up play dates for your sons with other good kids.

4. For older boys, encourage them to spend time with the kids you know are good.

---

[90] Li, et al. (2011)
[91] Gleason (2005)

5. For all ages, talk to your boys about what *makes* a good friend, as well as a bad one.

6. Talk to your boys about how they choose their friends and what they look for in their friendships.

7. Explain to your boys why certain so-called friends of theirs are probably not the best influence on their lives. Point out specific examples: "Remember when you hung out with Johnny and the two of you set fire to that old barn? It doesn't seem like you do that when you hang out with Bill."

8. Encourage your boys to police their own friendships and end the ones that are not positive.

> **TIP #029:** Monitor your boys' friends. Be an active participant in helping them choose and maintain their friendships.

> **TIP #030:** In some extreme cases, you might need to forbid your boys to spend time with certain kids. Be careful with this one—it can backfire on you. The thing that is forbidden is the thing your boys will want the most. Remember, you can catch more flies with honey than you can with vinegar.

As far as happiness is concerned, there is strong evidence from American and international research that empathy increases happiness.[92] The research is fairly clear—if boys' empathy and emotional regulation increase, so will their ability to gain friends, avoid victimization and bullying, and develop into happy, well-adjusted men.[93]

---

[92] Totan, el al. (2013); Tullett, et al. (2013); Wei, et al. (2011)
[93] Way & Silverman (2012)

In addition to better friends and increased happiness, empathy also leads to higher levels of confidence. Imagine for a moment that you are a new medical student and your instructor hands you your first syringe with the following instructions: "Give that patient a shot." Imagine you are a young adult whose first job is as a camp counselor for children infected with HIV. Picture yourself working in a prison and leading a support group for convicts. In all three of these intense and intimidating scenarios, there were links found between empathy and confidence.[94] More empathy leads to more confidence.

It turns out, boys who are empathic are going to be happier, have better friends, and they will experience more confidence in their abilities.

Improved conflict resolution skills

Empathy is closely linked to improved problem-solving skills for boys, and it does not keep boys from engaging in conflict.[95] By the time boys are adolescents, empathy helps them resolve conflicts with peers through active problem solving, and discourages escalating the conflict. But empathy *does not* cause boys to shy away from conflict or become overly passive or compliant. In short, they address conflict head on, in an effective and assertive manner, and they do not back down on their principles.

Even in preschoolers, the benefits of empathy and accuracy in reading the emotions of their peers is clear. As teenagers and adults, boys should not want to avoid conflict; they should be able to address it effectively and solve the underlying problems. But in preschoolers, conflict almost always leads to verbal or physical aggression. Empathic ability in preschoolers lowers the rate

---

94 Chunharas, et al. (2013); London, et al. (2013); Mariana (2013)
95 de Wied, et al. (2007)

of that conflict.[96] This finding only holds true for girls; of course, that is likely due to the different ways we socialize girls and boys. It is highly likely that male preschoolers would be just as good at avoiding conflict if we taught them at an early age how to understand what other people are feeling.

> **TIP #031:** If you want your boys to be leaders, if you want them to grow into mighty men, teach them to be empathic. They will be problem solvers and they will not shy away from conflict.

Better chances of getting into college and/or getting a job

Among other traits, empathy has been shown to predict success in college students for both male and female students.[97] In fact, one study from 2012 went so far as to demonstrate that the frontal lobes[98] of college students worked better for those students who were more empathic.[99]

In the workplace, research on empathy is just as clear. Doctors who are more empathic are more competent.[100] Engineers who are empathic are better problem solvers.[101] Empathic attorneys earn their clients more money.[102] Business leaders who are empathic make the best, and most ethical, business-related judgments,[103] despite business students consistently ranking empathy lowest in

---

[96] Verbeek (1997)
[97] Miley & Spinella (2007); Zienkewicz (2010)
[98] The part of the brain tasked with emotional regulation, impulse control, emotional regulation and higher-order thinking
[99] Puskar (2012)
[100] Hojat, et al. (2002)
[101] Nordfstrom & Korpelainen (2011)
[102] Elbers, et al. (2012)
[103] Natale & Sora (2010)

importance when presented with a list of leadership characteristics.[104] Salespeople who are empathic sell more.[105] Construction foremen who are empathic are better at their jobs.[106] Truck drivers who are empathic kill fewer horses on the side of the road.[107] [108]

> **TIP #032:** If you want your boys to do better in college, if you want them to do better at work, if you want their brains to literally work better, help them learn to become empathic and regulate their emotions. They will develop into strong, effective men.

Quicker identification of true mental health problems

The vast majority of boys can learn to regulate their emotions. They can develop empathy. They can control their behavior in most situations. However, there is a minority of boys who *can't* control their behavior. They *can't* learn to recognize how other kids are feeling. Those are the boys who might have true mental health problems that need to be diagnosed and treated.

There are numerous studies examining the relationship between different mental health conditions and lack of empathy and behavioral problems. For example, Attention Deficit/ Hyperactivity Disorder, commonly referred to as ADHD or ADD, is a cause of lack of empathic ability and behavioral problems in boys—their lack of attention affects their ability to recognize emotions in others and leads to a number of behavioral issues.[109]

---

[104] Holt & Marques (2012)
[105] Szyper-Perl (1969)
[106] Foa (1956)
[107] Seriously. This study actually exists. It's cited right there in the next footnote, and it is fairly recent.
[108] Chapman & Musselwhite (2011)
[109] Marton (2009); Uekermann, et al. (2010)

There are indications that the lack of empathy actually *causes* negative peer relationships in boys with ADHD.[110] Interestingly, and as an aside, boys with ADHD do better when their parents have empathy for their condition—not just a little better, but *considerably* better. The boys of empathic parents are less aggressive and more likely to have friends than are the boys whose parents do not understand their ADHD.[111]

> **TIP #033:** If you have a boy with ADHD, try to be as empathic as you can toward him. Let him know you understand where he is coming from, how he feels, and why he does the things he does. He will be better off for it. Raising a child with ADHD can be incredibly frustrating, and you will not be able to be empathic all of the time. Just do your best.

In addition to ADHD, people of all ages who are experiencing major depression have difficulty with frontal lobe tasks, including empathy.[112] The same is true of individuals who experience acute anxiety.[113] This finding is even stronger for individuals with Schizophrenia and Bipolar Disorder.[114]

> **TIP #034:** Schizophrenia is rare in children under the age of 18, and it is a disorder that is very difficult to treat. If you suspect your boy has a problem with psychotic thinking, it is extremely important that you get him examined as soon as possible.

Further, boys who are diagnosed with an autism spectrum disorder, which includes Asperger's Syndrome, have significant

---

[110] Cordier, et al. (2010)
[111] Warren (2004)
[112] Thoma, et al. (2011)
[113] Negd, et al. (2011)
[114] Derntl, et al. (2012)

difficulty with social relationships and empathy. In some cases, they cannot read other people's facial expressions and literally lack the neurological capacity for empathy.[115]

We know we can teach boys to be empathic and to regulate their emotions. We also know that a variety of mental illnesses can hinder a boy's ability to learn those important skills. It stands to reason then that if a boy is having trouble learning to be empathic, it might be due to parents who are trying their best but inadvertently using incorrect teaching techniques. It also may be due to a mental health problem.

If your boys are having difficulty learning how to be empathic and control their emotions, ask yourself these questions:

1. How old are the boys? Younger boys are going to have a harder time controlling their behavior, just because of their age. But they should be able to understand how to be empathic at a rudimentary level. Older boys should be able to learn these techniques in a much more sophisticated way. Your twelve year old should not be throwing temper tantrums.

2. How empathic have the boys' parents and/or caretakers been? Be honest with this question ... the less empathy shown toward your boys, the harder it will be for them to learn these techniques.

3. What is the boys' social environment like? Are they surrounded by negative influences?

4. What are your teaching strategies? Are you sure they are effective?

5. Do you think your boys might have issues with a mental health condition? ADHD, Depression, Anxiety, Bipolar Disorder, Schizophrenia, Autism/Asperger's? If you suspect

[115] Hirvela & Helkama (2011)

this is the case (and remember, poor socialization can mimic mental illness in boys—see Question #3 and re-ask yourself if you or someone you know is to blame), you should get your boys professionally evaluated.

> **TIP #035:** If your boys just don't seem to be able to be empathic, focus on the five questions listed above and think about having them professionally evaluated.

A random thought: self-control starts with empathy

In the review of research on empathy and emotional regulation in boys, one main theme emerged. Boys who are able to control their emotions and behaviors have good empathy skills. It seems that one of the major keys to keeping boys' emotions under control is making sure they are able to understand why others feel and act the way they do.[116]

At first, this idea might not make any sense. Keeping our own behaviors in check should have nothing to do with understanding how other people are feeling. But for a moment, imagine the following scenario: You are in a grocery store on a Saturday afternoon. The aisles are crowded; the carts are banging into one another, and there are long lines in the check-out lanes. You are frustrated because your shopping trip is taking longer than you thought it would. Then you turn a corner to head down the bread aisle and you see a mother yelling at her young son. She is angrily telling him to put the bread back because they don't need it and she is getting sick of him grabbing food off the shelves without asking. Now ... what are your thoughts about the mother?

---

[116] de Wied, et al. (2005) (2006); Marsh, et al. (2008); Wyatt (2002)

You might be thinking she is mean or abusive.[117] You might react with anger. You might want to confront her and tell her what a terrible parent she is. Even if you don't act on your anger, you are likely to stew on the thought of such an awful person being in charge of children for the rest of the day.

Now let's switch the scenario a bit. Picture the same exact scene in the same exact grocery store, except that when you come around the corner, the woman you see yelling at her child is a friend of yours. You know she's angry, and you know she's acting inappropriately, but you also know she just lost her job and is worried about losing her house. You know she's a good mother who is under a great deal of stress. And you also know the grocery store is not a fun place to be at the present time. Now ... what is your reaction?

There is a good chance you will not be as angry when you see her berating her child. You will understand the mental pain she is experiencing. You know her actions are over the top, but you might want to help. You might want to ask her if everything is okay. You might want to give her a hug. You might even want to offer to watch her son for a few minutes while she grabs whatever else she needs.

When you understand the emotions of others, and what is driving those feelings, you tend to react in a much healthier manner. And you are less likely to get angry.

It works for you, and it works for boys. Emotional regulation and positive behaviors often start with empathy.

> **TIP #036:** Recognize that understanding another person's situation helps you develop a more helpful reaction. So ask yourself this question: If it works for you, won't it work for your boys too?

---

[117] Have you ever had this thought: "If that's how she treats her kids in public, how much worse is it at home?"

Those are the benefits, but what are the drawbacks?

After a good deal of reflective thought, it seems that teaching boys to recognize and regulate their emotions, along with understanding the emotions of others, has many benefits. But it is important to reflect on potential drawbacks, as well. Remember, an important step in the reflective, critical thinking process is to look for evidence that disproves your theory.

This is where the fear raised at the beginning of this chapter might come into play: We will teach our boys to be girls. Arguments such as, "It's just in a boy's nature to be aggressive," come up over and over again. But as we learned from Chapter 2, this isn't necessarily so.

Yes, boys have testosterone to deal with, and that can cause life-long issues with aggression and problems with short-term aggression as well. They do sometimes have testosterone working against them when it comes to anger, aggression, and poor behavior. But they also have socialization working against them.

Remember the research—young girls and boys start out with roughly the same propensity toward violent outbursts, and we train that propensity out of girls. In boys, violence is rewarded, overlooked, or punished less harshly. And it is only the boys who have other environmental risk factors for problem behavior who have testosterone-related problems. For boys who are socialized in stable environments, higher levels of testosterone exposure actually leads to life-long benefits, such as leadership, high motivation, and a sense of fairness.[118]

---

[118] One of the risk factors for boys' misbehaving is growing up in poverty. Being born into poverty and escaping poverty, and its many negative effects, are issues that are largely out of a human being's control. I do not mean to imply that poor parents are not as good as parents who live a financially comfortable life. Instead, it is important to recognize that some

This is another common argument against teaching boys to be more emotionally mature: "If you are empathic and emotional, you can't be assertive. People will walk all over you." This is a tempting argument, but its roots are based in fear—fear that our boys will be pushovers, weak and emotional.

But, which is harder—getting angry or taking the time to fully understand a situation and work toward a fair solution? Anger is easy. Hippos can get angry.[119] Dogs can get angry. Any simple-minded person can throw a temper tantrum and punch a wall. That is not strength. That is the easy response.

By contrast, *empathy* is hard. *Emotional restraint* is hard. *Understanding* is hard. *Reflection* is hard. Aren't those the qualities we want in our society's men? If we want our boys to be *all boy*, we do *not* want to teach them to take the easy, limited, and frequently ineffective path.

Instead of the easy way, try to address the issue the hard way. The strong way. The mighty way. Talk to your son about what he is doing. Talk to him about *why* it is wrong. Ask him why he is doing it. Ask him if his behavior is improving his life or making it worse. Ask him how it makes him feel. Explain how his behavior makes other people feel. If need be, punish him. But make sure he *understands* why he is being punished.

Here is another potential argument against socializing our boys differently: "My parents didn't do that for me, and I turned out okay." Unless you are reading this book in prison,[120] you are

---

causes of boys' behavioral problems are completely within parents' control and others are not.

[119] In fact, despite their depiction in most cartoons, hippos are amongst the angriest of mammals. They kill more humans every year than sharks. In fact, sharks don't even make the top twenty. Sharks with lasers on their heads are a different story, however.

[120] If you are reading this in prison, allow me to suggest a different book. Possibly *Man's Search For Meaning* by Viktor Frankl. See the reference section for more details.

probably right—you are most likely fine. Most men get along well in life, treating others with respect and asking for respect in return. Even so, there are still alarming numbers of men who are arrested every year for domestic violence, rape, assault, and murder. There are captains of industry who make decisions based on short-term profit rather than the betterment of humanity. There are politicians who routinely bring our country to the brink of disaster. There are men in power who assume conflicts can only be resolved through war. We should be able to do better than that.

And on an individual level, isn't it important to think about what you can change about yourself to improve your life? Are you sure you couldn't be doing better in your relationships? At your job? With your family? If there is solid scientific research that points to a solution that would give your sons a huge advantage, wouldn't you want to take advantage of that research?

They'll do better in school; they'll do better in their jobs, and they'll have more friends. They'll be happier. They'll have a strong sense of fairness. They'll deal with conflict in a healthier way. They'll learn there are ways to confront others that do not require anger or violence. They'll be more assertive. They won't back down from a fight, and they won't fight with their fists. They'll achieve more. They'll lead. They'll improve the world.

Or you can teach your boys to be weak and take the easy way out. You can worry about their manliness and disguise fear with tradition. It's up to you.

Wait a minute ... did this book just insult people who disagree with it?

Oops. It did. It basically called parents who don't agree with the premise of the book a bunch of backward leaning, fear-filled, child-hating idiots. Not exactly the most empathic, emotionally-regulated way to make a point, is it? Especially in a book that extols the virtues of emotional regulation, empathic understanding, and treating others with respect. It seems ironic that it has broken its own rules. As such, the book apologizes deeply if it has offended you.[121]

But maybe I can use this lapse in judgment as a teaching moment. Certainly, the point can be made that there are many objections parents of both genders will have to teaching boys to be more emotionally mature and empathic. Some of those reasons are rooted in fear, and others are not. But it is important to understand *why* parents object. Not just the reasons why they object, but the reasons *behind the reasons*. In many cases, the fear is that their boys will be too ineffective and be taken advantage of as a result.

This is a valid fear. Of course every decent parent is going to want his or her boys to be safe and happy. All parents want their boys to grow into stable, mature men. No one wants a boy to be taken advantage of. *Of course.* These fears and concerns are perfectly understandable. They are even commendable.

And the good news is that teaching your boys emotional stability and empathy skills will help you achieve your goals for them. As we have learned in this chapter, there are numerous benefits of empathy in boys, some of which should allay parents' fears— empathy can actually make boys *more* effective when in conflict with others, *more* fair, and *more* leader-like. It will not make them weaker!

> **TIP #037:** Teach your boys to be strong. Give them the opportunity to benefit from your turning out okay—use your stability as a springboard for them to achieve even more. Shed the worry that teaching your boys emotional maturity will turn them into girls. The advantages they

---

[121] Sincerely, I am sorry.

will gain by learning those traditionally feminine characteristics will make them stronger men—or more appropriately, it will make them stronger people.

Now, you may still have doubts, and these last several paragraphs may not have convinced you, but you at least have to admit they didn't insult you. The intention was to give a real-time example of what empathy might look like, how it might feel, and how it is likely to work better than antagonism and brow beating.

> **TIP #038:** Think about which approach you liked better—condescension, anger, and authoritarianism ... or, empathy, understanding, and explanation. Which do you think would work better for your boys? Which do you think would make them stronger?

CHAPTER 4

I Learned It By Watching You: your boys will know if you have no idea what you are talking about

"Have you ever seen a rhino pee?"

I actually asked my kids this question at dinner once. I don't know why. It just came out. We were talking about rhinoceroses, and I thought that this question would add richness to the conversation.[122] My kids were fascinated as I described how long it takes a rhino to empty its bladder and how gross it is to see them standing in their own urine. Remember, we were eating dinner at the time.

To my wife's dismay, the kids talk about gross stuff while we are eating. It bothers her, and I don't blame her. And it's my fault. I taught them that it's okay to discuss unappetizing topics while eating. They learned it by watching me.

You can't fool your boys. They will watch what you do, and they will imitate it—whether you want them to or not.

---

[122] If you ever get the chance to watch a rhino peeing, I suggest you do it. They must have bladders the size of gas tanks. They just go and go and go.

If you smoke, your boys are more likely to smoke—even when you tell them it is bad for them. When you quit smoking, your boys are still less likely to listen to you when you tell them not to pick up the habit.[123] If you have unhealthy eating habits, your boys will too—regardless of what you tell them about healthy eating.[124] Same goes with exercise,[125] television,[126] drugs and alcohol,[127] and just about everything else you can imagine.[128] Put yourself in their shoes—think back to when you were a kid. You knew what your parents were doing. If they were telling you to do something differently from the way they were doing it, did you listen to them?

In psychology, this phenomenon is referred to as *modeling*, and as a teaching technique, it is very powerful. Whether we like it or not, our boys will learn how to interact with the world by watching our behavior and imitating us—most often without even realizing they are doing it. In fact, that is the definition of modeling as a behavioral technique: to teach someone a behavior by having him watch and imitate someone else. It really does work, and it does not matter if the student has any idea what is transpiring.[129]

> **TIP #039:** Walk the talk. If you want your boys to do something (or avoid doing something), model the proper behavior. They will follow your lead, and they will spot hypocrisy—even if they never verbalize it.

---

[123] Kodl & Mermelstein (2004); McGee, et al. (2006)
[124] Blom-Hoffman (2001); Wrotniak, et al. (2005)
[125] DiLorenzo, et al. (1998); Rhodes, et al. (2010)
[126] He, et al. (2010)
[127] King, et al. (2003)
[128] This includes discussions of rhino micturation.
[129] If you don't believe me, talk about rhino pee at the dinner table and see what happens. I really can't emphasize this point enough.

There are hundreds of studies showing the power of modeling and highlighting its effectiveness. The most famous of these studies were Albert Bandura's 'Bobo doll experiments' from the 1960s. If you remember from previous chapters, Bandura essentially taught children to become aggressive by having them watch adults acting aggressively. The effects did not necessarily last, but it was the beginning of understanding how children learn through imitating adults.

In the years that followed, hundreds of researchers have shown that modeling can teach positive behaviors as well as negative ones. For example, modeling pro-social imitative behaviors is now a normal part of the treatment of autism, and more recently, video modeling has been incorporated into this type of treatment.[130] Interestingly, boys can even learn new social skills by modeling *their own behavior*—their behavior can improve after observing examples of their own good deeds on video and receiving feedback on it.[131]

> **TIP #040:** With the advent of video recorders on smart phones, most parents have a ton of video of their children doing all sorts of things. If you happen to catch your boys doing something good on video, show it to them, explain to them why it is good, and praise them for it.

> **TIP #041:** Don't stalk your boys with your phone in an attempt to catch them doing something good. That will most likely freak them out.

In an older study[132] that separated modeling into two different tasks—imitation and observation—researchers discovered something interesting, especially in younger children. It turns out that boys between the ages of four and seven learn through modeling

---

[130] Boudreau & D'Entremont (2010); Rayner (2011)
[131] Calpin & Cinciripini (1980); Wert & Neisworth (2003)
[132] Even older than me.

differently, based on their age. In the study, the younger children learned new behaviors through actively *imitating* an adult—copying what the adult was doing. But as they aged, boys' need to learn through imitation decreased. They were able to learn new behaviors merely by *observing* an adult. This finding suggests that, as boys get older, the power of modeling as a learning tool grows stronger. Boys do not need to copy us exactly to learn new skills or bad habits; instead, they will learn those good skills or poor habits just by watching us.[133]

> **TIP #042:** By the age of seven, your boys only need to watch you to learn bad habits, so be careful what you do and say around them.

> **TIP #043:** On the other hand, your boys will quickly be able to learn good social and life skills just by watching you, so you have the capacity to send them powerful messages about how to grow into psychologically healthy adults just by acting like a good human being in their presence.

Model the behavior you want your boys to exhibit

As we now know, if they see it, they will learn to do it. So we need to do it right. Since the rhino incident, I have stopped talking about disgusting topics during dinner. My kids have not yet followed suit. Remember the study mentioned at the beginning of this chapter? The one that showed that the boys of smokers are more likely to start smoking, even if they see their parents quit? Well, the same may be true of potty talk.

In the context of this book, *doing it right* means teaching your boys to understand and regulate their emotions and to have

---

[133] Hermanns & De Winther (1971)

empathy for others. In a modeling paradigm, that means you need to understand and regulate *your* emotions. That means *you* need to have empathy for others. Remember, your boys will learn from your behavior and unless you want to hear the words of the most famous public service announcement of all time (*"You! All right? I learned it by watching you!"*[134]), you should probably learn how to use the emotional skills you will be asking your boys to develop.

> **TIP #044:** If you want to teach your boys to be emotionally mature, let them learn by watching you.

Learn to understand, and then regulate, your emotions

Before you can truly grasp how others are feeling and why they are feeling that way, it is important to understand your own emotional reactions. If you understand your emotions and put them into larger perspective, it becomes much easier to control those emotions. You don't have to fly into a rage—you can experience frustration instead. You don't need to burst into tears during a sad commercial—you can feel sadness and sympathy for the people in the advertisement.

In other words, you need to be able to have empathy for yourself. Then you can have empathy for others.

The full development of understanding where your emotions are coming from and why you are feeling them is an incremental process. By taking small steps, you move yourself toward fuller

---

[134] If you don't know what I am talking about, take a break from reading and search "I learned it by watching you" on YouTube. The first video will be a PSA from 1987. As an added bonus, you will get to see a kid listening to a stereo with actual knobs plugged into an actual outlet.

knowledge of your motivations. The steps are fairly simple ... *carrying them out* is a little more challenging.

First, here are the steps to understanding your emotions, in question form:

1. What emotion are you experiencing?

2. What is the most immediate cause of that emotion?

3. Why did that immediate cause result in the particular emotion you are feeling, as opposed to a different emotion?

4. What other factors, besides the immediate cause, led you to experience the emotion you are feeling?

5. How can you assess, and potentially dispute, those other factors and make a positive change?

Before breaking down these steps/questions into actual actions, let me apply them to a fictional, but not uncommon, scenario. Here is the scene:

You are late for work.[135] It took you longer than normal to get your boys out of the house for school. They were just in one of those moods—totally uncooperative. You had to threaten to send them to school in their pajamas, which finally did the trick. In the meantime, you are late. If you speed a little more than usual and run a few more yellowish lights, you could probably get there on time. Usually, you get there with a few minutes to spare ... and you hate being late.

Your anxiety is running high as you get into your car. It squeals to a start—a stark reminder that you need to have someone check the engine. You don't have time now, so you decide to think about scheduling an appointment at lunch today.

You leave your neighborhood and are on the main thoroughfare to work—the one with all the stoplights. Traffic is moving

---

[135] I am not sure how common this is for you, but it is a fairly frequent occurrence in the Wachtel household.

slower than you want it to, and you find yourself tapping on the steering wheel and lunging forward in your seat as you weave in and out of traffic. You know you are driving a little too aggressively, but you have an excuse: You hate being late. Normally you are a safe and courteous driver.

It is right when you finish this thought that a driver swerves in front of you. You quickly realize that you are in this driver's blind spot, and he can't see you. Even so, he is swerving into your lane too quickly, and he isn't even using his turn signal.

You slam on your breaks. You weave to the right side of your lane. You look in the rear-view mirror to see if anyone is going to hit you from behind.

And then everything is fine.

There is no accident. No one dies. The swerving driver is now in front of you, talking on his phone, and he has no idea what he has done. You—on the other hand—are beside yourself with rage.

In that moment, ask yourself these questions.

1. **What is the emotion you are feeling?**

This is almost always an easy question to answer. If you spend a few seconds thinking about your feelings, you can typically come up with a ready answer. In this case, we know what you are feeling: anger. Not just anger, though. More intense than anger. You are feeling rage. Say the following sentence to yourself right now:

"I am feeling enraged."

> **TIP #045:** A feeling statement ("I am feeling
> _____") is the beginning of empathy.

2. **What is the most immediate cause of that emotion?**

This one is not always as easy to answer as question #1, but it is typically pretty simple as well. In this case, you are enraged because a man cut you off in traffic and could have caused a major accident. Add to the original answer:

"I am feeling enraged because a man cut me off and almost caused an accident."

> **TIP #046:** The longer feeling statement ("I am feeling enraged because a man cut me off and almost caused an accident") is basic empathy. It acknowledges the feeling and the reason behind the feeling. This is one of the first techniques beginning counselors learn, only they direct it toward others. As in, "You are feeling enraged because a man cut you off and almost caused an accident." There is obviously much more to counseling than repeating this empathic phrase over and over again ("You feel _____ because _____"), but that is where it all starts.[136]

3. **Why did that immediate cause result in the particular emotion you are feeling, as opposed to a different emotion?**

Why did you become enraged? Why didn't you experience another emotion? In some cases, this question is easy to answer—you did not feel happiness because that would be ridiculous. No one would be happy after a near-collision. But why didn't you feel sad? Or frustrated? Or confused? Or terrified? Your go-to emotion in this instance was rage, even though other people might have experienced a very different type of emotion.

In part, understanding your emotional reaction to an event requires a deeper understanding of how people form emotions in general. There has been a lot of research in this area over the

---

[136] A quick search on PsychInfo, the leading compendium of psychological research, reveals thousands of studies demonstrating a link between therapist empathy and therapeutic effectiveness.

past 50 years, and psychologists now have a reasonable grasp of the process.

From a purely biological perspective, there are only a limited number of emotions that humans are capable of experiencing. Sometimes referred to as *innate emotions*, these are the feeling states that are hardwired into our brains. They include excitement, fear, anger, sadness, and love. And that's about it. The vast majority of our brain is similar to that of every other mammal on the planet, and we all have a biologically limited ability to express emotion.

What is more, the physiological processes associated with the first three of these innate emotions—excitement, fear, and anger—are exactly the same. When we are terrified, our heart rate increases, we sweat, we widen our eyes, we lose the ability to concentrate on anything other than what is causing our fear. We need to urinate. We need to get up and run away ... or we freeze ... or we want to engage physically with whatever it is that is causing our fear. And the same exact thing happens when we are excited. We interpret our physiological reactions in a very different way because we are happy instead of scared, but our bodies react in the same way. Anger is no different. Sadness and love *are* different, however, in that they tend to cause physiological functions that slow our bodies down rather than speed them up.[137]

So the question about why you did not react to the car accident situation with happiness suddenly does not seem so ridiculous. Your body doesn't know the physiological difference between happiness, anger, and fear. So why didn't you react with happiness?

The answer to this question is rooted in the part of our brain that differentiates us from other animals—the frontal lobe and prefrontal cortex. As discussed in previous chapters, this is the

---

[137] Actually, love is a mixed bag. It calms us, but we also experience physiological reactions (such as racing heart) when we are first developing a loving attraction to someone else. This is often thought of as sexual excitement instead of love, however.

thin outer covering of the brain (toward the front of our heads) that helps us to think clearly. It also helps us interpret and regulate our emotions.[138]

So, when you are in your car, already having a bad day, and a man cuts you off, nearly causing an accident, the structures deep inside your brain take action. They dump a bunch of chemicals into your system that cause your body to rev up, and you experience a basic, innate emotion. But it is the thinking part of your brain that causes you to interpret those bodily reactions as rage instead of excitement.

Because of your highly developed brain, you quickly take into account the frustrations of your day and the circumstances of the incident—the man in front of you nearly killed you, and you were already having a bad day. Your body is racing, and of course you are going to feel enraged. It is just basic biology, right?

Right. Except that humans are capable of many more emotions than happiness, anger, and fear. A quick Internet search will produce hundreds of words used to describe different emotional states.

> **TIP #047:** Enter the phrase "words for emotions" into your favorite Internet search engine and expand your *emotional vocabulary*. Think for a few moments about the subtle differences between certain emotions. For example, what is the real difference between the following words: hateful, scornful, spiteful, and vengeful?[139] They all are a form of anger that includes lingering vindictiveness, but each is slightly different.

---

[138] It is also the part of our brains that we smack into the windshield when we are in an accident and not wearing a seat belt.
[139] Retrieved from www.wire.wisc.edu

Researchers refer to the complex feeling states that stem from innate emotions as *biocultural emotions*.[140] Our complex emotional states are driven by our innate biological processes and our limited ability to experience emotion, but they are also affected by our environment. Rather than feeling rage, we can use the thinking part of our brain to experience a wide range of subtle, culturally appropriate and effective emotions.

So now, the initial question should be more meaningful: Why did you experience rage after the man cut you off in traffic? Why did you stop at that basic, innate emotion? That is essentially what rats do. In fact, rats are able to use their tiny frontal cortices to regulate their tiny, innate emotions.[141] But you are smarter than a rat, and your brain is a lot bigger.

> **TIP #048:** Remember you are smarter than a rat. Now think about why it is that you allowed yourself to stop at "rage" in the car scenario, or in other real examples from your life. Typically, it is because feeling the innate emotion is easy. Your body is primed to feel one of a limited number of intense emotions, and it takes absolutely no conscious brainpower to get angry, or sad, or scared, or excited.

> **TIP #049:** Try putting some conscious thought into why you are feeling the way you are feeling. Use your frontal cortex, and that list of emotion words you looked up earlier, to gain a more sophisticated grasp of your emotional capacity. You don't have to feel *enraged*. You can feel aggravated, or grumpy, or exasperated, or hurt. These are all biocultural variations of enraged that allow you to experience the full range of

---

[140] Engelen, et al. (2009); Matsumoto & Hwang (2012)
[141] Chan, et al. (2011)

human possibility without needing to mindlessly resort to a 'fight, flight, or freeze' response.

TIP #050: When you learn to use your full brain and experience subtle variations in biocultural emotions, you can teach your boys to do it too. In fact, merely modeling this ability is sometimes enough for boys to learn to start thinking with their brains and not their fists. This is especially true when, as the parent, you believe that teaching your boys to regulate their emotional lives is important and you provide strong role modeling in this area.[142]

4. What other factors, besides the immediate cause, led you to experience the emotion you are feeling?

Face it: You are safe. There is no real reason to be feeling rage. What else could be causing your heightened emotions?

Let's review the facts. You were running late. Your boys were driving you crazy. Your car needs work, and you are worried about how to pay for the repairs. Traffic was moving slowly. The driver in front of you didn't even notice that he *almost* killed someone.

All of those are excellent reasons to be temporarily flustered. But the question you need to ask is, "Why was I filled with rage?"

In order to answer this question, it is important to understand one of the central concepts behind Cognitive Behavioral Therapy, one of the most commonly used modern therapeutic techniques in the world. The essence of this type of therapy lies in understanding how our thoughts are responsible for our emotions and our behavior. And by recognizing our thoughts—even those that happen so deep in our unconscious we do not realize they are

---

[142] Liag, et al. (2012)

there—we can understand and change how we react in all kinds of negative situations.[143]

The cognitive behavioral key to recognizing the underlying thoughts beneath the specific causes of our negative reactions is to determine whether those thoughts are rational or irrational. Simply put, rational thoughts lead to rational emotions. Irrational thoughts lead to irrational emotions.[144]

So, what are the underlying thoughts in the car example? If they are so ingrained that we don't realize we are thinking them, how can we learn to recognize and change them? The easiest way to do this is to let someone else do most of the work for you. In this case, noted cognitive behavioral psychologist Albert Ellis[145] listed twelve common irrational thoughts that get in peoples' way. They are listed in his book, titled *The Practice of Rational Emotive Behavior Therapy*, and I will summarize them here:[146]

4.1   Important people in my life need to love me for everything I do.

4.2   Certain actions are evil or wicked and the people who commit them are terrible humans.

4.3   It is terrible when things are not the way I want them to be.

4.4   Human suffering is always caused by external factors forced on me by others.

4.5   If something is scary or dangerous, I need to fret about it constantly.

---

[143] Beck (1976); Ellis & Dryden (1997)
[144] Ellis (1962)
[145] 1913-2007
[146] Ellis & Dryden (1997) Please remember, this list is not something I created. I wish I could take credit for it, but it is a result of Dr. Ellis's hard work—not mine.

4.6 It is easier for me to avoid life's difficulties than to face them.

4.7 I need something/someone stronger than me on which to rely for stability in my life.

4.8 I need to be perfect in all respects.

4.9 Because something strongly affected me before, it will strongly affect my life forever.

4.10 I must have perfect control over everything.

4.11 I can achieve happiness by doing nothing.

4.12 I have no control over my emotions and I can't help but get upset by certain things.

TIP #051: Read through Dr. Ellis's list and see if any of the 12 ideas rings true for you.

Using the car example, you can determine if any of Dr. Ellis's irrational ideas might be at work. For example, he argues that people commonly believe there are some actions that are inherently evil and people who engage in those actions are absolutely terrible people. In some cases this might be true—think of murder, terrorism, sexual assault, and so on. But under most circumstances, it is irrational to think a person who does something wrong is completely evil. Sure, the guy who cut you off in traffic did something very dangerous, but chances are, he is a good person who may be having an equally bad day. Perhaps you can cut him a break.

Another of Dr. Ellis's common thoughts is that we must have perfect control over every aspect of our lives. That particular thought is a recipe for disaster. There is so much that is out of our control that we are going to be miserable every time something bad happens when we try to control everything. You can scream at your boys until you burst a blood vessel in your eye, but it is not going to speed them up some mornings. You are better off understanding this and being okay with giving up some control.

One last irrational thought Dr. Ellis listed is that we have almost no control over our emotions and can't help feeling upset about some things. This is just not true. You do have control over how you react to situations, and there is no inherent reason why you need to fly into a blind rage when someone cuts you off in traffic. Stop thinking that you have no control over your emotions. In fact, going back to Dr. Ellis's previous point about having little control over what happens in life, our emotional reaction to events is one of the few areas where we *do* have the capacity for complete control.

> **TIP #052:** After you recognize the irrational thoughts that under-gird your negative reactions, think about how you can regain control of your life and your emotions.

5. How can you assess and potentially dispute those other factors and make a positive change?

Once you understand the emotions you are feeling, and the deep, underlying reasons for them, you have the ability to change your reaction. In cognitive behavioral terms, you must *dispute* the irrational thought that is causing your negative emotion.

> **TIP #053:** One word of warning: Not all negative emotions are irrational. Feeling depressed after the death of a loved one is rational. Being terrified when being chased by a bear is rational. Experiencing rage in traffic is not rational.

The key to disputing your irrational beliefs, assuming they are causing negative consequences in your life, is to think through the situation rationally. In the car scenario, you are able to realize it is normal to have a heightened physiological reaction to the stress of almost getting into an accident. That will naturally cause you to feel some anxiety and anger. But you must also realize you were having a bad day—it was your fault you were running late, and to make up for it, you tried to take control of too many external factors. Instead of calling work and explaining you would be a few minutes late, you left it up to fate to try to make up for lost time, and fate was not on your side. Even though the man swerved in front of you and could have caused a potentially dangerous accident, he is probably not a bad person, and thank goodness, no one was hurt.

After having these realizations, your emotional reaction may be different. Instead of flying into a rage, you can take several deep breaths, realize you were being irrational, and slowly allow the natural anxiety you are feeling to diminish. Instead of allowing it to ruin your day, and potentially exposing your boys (who are in the backseat) to unnecessary rage,[147] you can calm down and tell yourself there are more important issues on which you can spend your energy.

> **TIP #054:** Recognizing and disputing irrational beliefs goes a long way toward helping you control your emotions and teaching your boys how to do it.

Summary: modeling and teaching combine to great effect

As we have learned earlier in the chapter, boys can learn pro-social behaviors by watching and imitating their parents. And boys hate hypocrisy. In fact, "Do as I say, not as I do" is a completely useless

---

[147] Remember, modeling is an effective way to teach your boys. If you fly into a rage in traffic, your boys will learn that is acceptable behavior.

phrase. If you don't want your sons to smoke, don't smoke.[148] If you don't want them to eat unhealthy food, don't eat unhealthy food.[149] If you don't want them to use drugs, don't use drugs.[150]

It stands to reason that you should not expect your boys to recognize and regulate their emotions if you cannot do it yourself. And trying to explain to them how to control themselves when they see you fly into a rage after a near-miss car incident is a waste of time.

By the teen years, hypocrisy is a major source of conflict for boys.[151] Teenage boys become extremely upset and point out hypocrisy, even when it comes to the clothes they wear. In the 1990s, one school attempted to enforce a mandatory school uniform policy that they insisted was *voluntary*. Needless to say, the boys flipped out.[152]

Why would we expect our boys to give us a pass on telling them to control their emotions when we clearly have a problem doing so ourselves?

An interesting side-note to the research on boys and their dislike of parental hypocrisy is that they also dislike hypocrisy in themselves. Children inherently desire consistent behavior. Boys as young as age seven can be convinced to improve their behavior by teaching them pro-social behaviors and pointing out instances in the past where they failed to behave appropriately.[153]

> **TIP #055:** If you want your boys to improve their behavior, provide them with instances from the past where they failed to follow your rules for acceptable behavior. If you have taught them why your rules are important, and have lovingly

148 Schuck, et al. (2012)
149 Elfhag, et al. (2010)
150 Fleming, et al. (1997)
151 Buzzetta (2012)
152 Davidson-Williams (1997)
153 Morrongiello & Mark (2008)

pointed out instances in the past where they have fallen short, your boys will want to reduce their future hypocrisy by complying with the rules. IMPORTANT NOTE: The goal is not to shame your boys or to make them feel guilty. Make sure to point out to them that they are good kids and that you know they want to follow the rules, even though they fail sometimes.

In this chapter, you have read about the steps necessary to recognize, understand, and regulate your emotions. Practicing these skills makes the task easier, and both you and your boys will benefit greatly from your effort. Your boys will see you reacting calmly in a variety of situations. But sometimes your behavior may not be readily observable. For example, it is hard to actively observe a person *not reacting*.

Your boys might see you control your emotions well in a stressful situation, such as the car scenario. But all they will really see is you remaining calm and taking a few deep breaths. They will not be able to directly observe you working through your healthy thought process—recognizing your emotions, understanding why you are feeling them, identifying irrational ideas, and disputing those ideas. In order to fully teach your boys how to recognize and control their emotions, you will need to be able to do it yourself and then explain to them what you did.

In a series of fascinating studies from the 1970s and 1980s, researchers discovered this modeling-teaching technique actually works. If you model behaviors to boys and teach them a strategy for behaving well at the same time, they respond much better than if you just model good behavior. Even more impressive is that boys will also be able to take that strategy and use it in a variety of different situations—especially when they see you doing so.

This modeling-teaching technique works for boys as young as age four—an age where it is normally difficult for a child to learn a rule and apply it in different situations. It works with children with developmental disabilities, and it works with normally functioning children. Modeling and teaching works, and it works very, very well.[154] When you add an explanation to your action, the modeling effect increases and it is much more likely that your boys will imitate your pro-social behavior.[155]

> **TIP #056:** Don't just model good emotional regulation for your boys. Explain to them what you are doing and why you are doing it. They will respond positively to it—even at a very young age.

---

[154] Fields (1989); Zimmerman (1974)
[155] Hay, et al. (1985)

CHAPTER 5

Teach Like The Pros: 10 effective teaching techniques to help your boys recognize and regulate their emotions (Plus 5 Bonus Techniques)[156]

Now that you have the tools you need to understand and regulate your emotions, it is time to pass this knowledge on to your boys. This is not an easy task; figuring out how to do it yourself is tough. It will take a lot of patience, a lot of practice, and a lot of mistakes. And then you have to teach your boys how to do it.

The good news is that they have been watching you work hard at it. If you are modeling appropriate behavior, your boys will learn from you. If you are explaining to them what you are doing, including your struggles when you make a mistake, that will increase the likelihood that they will pick up some new skills without you doing a whole lot of extra work.

> **TIP #057:** Model appropriate emotional regulation behavior for your boys, and explain to them how you do it. Let them know when you've made

---

[156] That is 15 techniques!

a mistake, so they understand they don't have to
be perfect.

It seems like this chapter could end here. You have the knowledge from Chapter 4, and you merely need to impart it to your sons. But that is easier said than done. It is hard to be an effective teacher, and that task is often more difficult when you are related to your students.[157] Have you ever noticed how your boys respond to their schoolteachers telling them what to do differently than they respond when you do it? That is partially due to the different roles schoolteachers and parents play in the life of boys. But it is also due to the fact that schoolteachers are highly trained professionals who understand how to impart information in an impactful manner.

Here is a list of 10 strategies teachers learn that can help you share information with your sons:

1. Reflect on your teaching skills: Did your techniques work?

2. Give yourself the freedom to try new parenting techniques.

3. Help your sons take responsibility for learning how to control their emotions and have empathy toward others.

4. Don't stop learning how to recognize and control your emotions, and don't give up on learning new ways of teaching this to your boys. Same goes with developing empathy toward others.

5. Help your boys believe they are the ones doing the hard work, not you. It may not feel like it sometimes, but the truly engaged student is always working harder than the teacher.

---

[157] Don't even get me started on the frustration I experienced trying to teach my kids to ride a bike. They both figured it out—despite my best efforts.

6. Have your boys critique other people's emotional regulation and empathy abilities.

7. Engage your boys in active learning, not passive learning.

8. Give your boys a quiz every now and then.

9. Provide feedback to your sons as quickly as possible.

10. Continuously work on developing a positive relationship between you and your boys.

As you read this chapter, think about how you might be able to naturally work some of these teaching techniques into your day. You don't want to annoy your sons with the information in this book, and it is important to talk about things other than empathy with them.[158] You want them to grow into strong adults, but you want them to have a little fun along the way.

Here is the list of techniques again, along with some explanation:

1. **Reflect on your teaching skills: Did your techniques work?**

There is that skill again: reflective thinking. Rather than simply walking through life blindly, evaluating how well you are doing through reflection makes a huge difference. And you are putting a lot of effort into understanding your own emotions, modeling proper behavior to your sons, and explaining to them what you are doing. Wouldn't it be nice if you had some idea whether or not all your effort is working?

Beginning teachers quickly learn the importance of continually evaluating their teaching methods. As an example, imagine a math teacher employing several new teaching methods to teach her students geometry theorems. She has a good idea that those

---

[158] I recommend discussing frogs, sports, and television at least part of the time ... and rhino urination semi-annually.

teaching methods will work, but she wants to make sure she is not wasting her time, and—more importantly—her students' time. If those new strategies don't work, she can refine them or try something completely different. So she gives her students a test. She measures the students' performance on the test to see if her teaching strategies worked. She also compares each individual student's test performance to the student's last test performance, to see if each student learned more with her new teaching strategies. She uses that information to reflect on her performance and discovers that 10 of her 15 students answered more questions correctly on the latest test when compared with the previous test, but that five students did worse. She realizes she can make some changes to the new teaching methods to help *all* of her students improve, and she tries the strategies again in the next unit.

What educational research shows very clearly is that this type of reflection works.[159] And if you don't believe how often teachers use this technique, mention something about reflection the next time you are talking to your son's teacher. That person's eyes will light up, and you will get a dissertation on its importance in his or her daily teaching routine.[160]

By focusing on how you teach your sons, and whether or not it works, you can refine your skills and improve your sons' ability to learn from you.

Here are a few questions you can ask yourself when reflecting on your teaching effectiveness:

1.a   In the last 24 hours, have I seen any change in my sons' behavior? How about the last week? The last month?

1.b   Are my sons interested in what I am teaching them? Are they paying attention? Are they asking questions about it?

---

[159] Jove (2011)

[160] This is especially true in my kids' school where it's like, "Reflection this" and "Reflection that."

1.c   Are my sons talking about their emotions? Are they recognizing how they feel and discussing it with me? Are they recognizing emotions in others and understanding better where others are coming from?

1.d   Do my sons display the behaviors I have been attempting to model to them?

1.e   Do my sons seem less angry than before?

> **TIP #058:** Reflecting on your teaching by examining how you taught your sons, and comparing that to how well they are responding, will help you hone your skills. You will be able to quickly identify what is working and what needs to be adjusted.

2. **Give yourself the freedom to try new parenting techniques.**

If you empower yourself to learn some new techniques for raising your boys, your teaching skills will improve. It is okay to experiment a bit, looking for the best way to teach your sons how to recognize and regulate their emotions. Some of what you try will work very well. Some of it will fail. Some techniques will work well for one boy but will work terribly for another. The finest school principals know that kids learn best when they empower their teachers to learn new strategies, try those new strategies without the fear of losing their jobs, and reflect on how effective those new strategies are.[161]

So cut yourself some slack. No one is going to fire you from your parenting job. Try some new techniques and see how they work for you.

---

[161] Thoonen, et al. (2011)

TIP #059: It is important for you to be motivated to learn how to teach this information to your boys, and to feel like you have the power to do so. Your teaching ability will improve if you feel like you can experiment with how best to impart information to your sons, and then reflect on the outcome of those so-called experiments without judgment.

3. **Help your sons take responsibility for learning how to control their emotions and have empathy toward others.**

When teachers give students the responsibility for directing their learning, those students learn very well. To do this, teachers work with students to set appropriate goals and encourage them to take the lead in achieving those goals. What happens in situations like these is that students feel excited about learning and are motivated to improve.[162]

Obviously, you will need to tailor your teaching methods to the age of your boys. But it is possible, with some help and guidance, to teach a boy as young as three or four how to set goals to improve his behavior (for example, a simple goal would be to avoid getting a timeout for the next two days by recognizing when he is angry and taking several deep breaths). In general, the teaching strategies are highly similar, regardless of age. Here are some tips you can use to get your sons to take responsibility for their learning:

3.a   Have a discussion with your boys about the tangible benefits they have experienced when they have controlled their emotions. Ask them to think of a time when they were able to control their anger and help them reflect on why it was better for them to do so.

---

162 Ferguson (2009)

Help them come up with instances when having empathy toward someone else changed the way they reacted to a stressful/angering situation. If they need help, give them examples from your own life to get them started.

3.b Talk to them about appropriate goals for improving their emotional regulation and understanding of others. As much as you can, have your sons take the lead in this discussion. For younger boys, or boys who are more resistant to the idea of change, you will need to be more directive at this stage. The goals should be small and achievable. For example, "I won't ever get mad again" is a terrible goal. First, it is impossible to achieve. Second, it is not very tangible. A better goal would be, "I won't let my anger get out of control tomorrow," or "I will stop myself before overreacting at school next week and try to think about how the other person is feeling before I say anything."

3.c Help your sons refine the goals they have developed, and write down those goals.

3.d Encourage your sons to take responsibility for meeting their goals. Explain to them that you will help remind them of the goals and the methods they can use to achieve them, but you cannot control their behavior. They are the only ones who are fully able to achieve their goals.

3.e Reflect with your sons on whether or not they achieved their goals. If they have, praise them and help them set new ones. If they haven't, work with them to figure out what they need to do differently next time.

> **TIP #060:** Help your boys reflect on what they have learned; have them set goals for improving their emotional regulation and empathy abilities, and encourage them to take responsibility for achieving those goals. If you do so, they will learn more, and their behavior will improve.

4. **Don't stop learning about how to recognize and control your emotions, and don't give up on learning new ways of teaching this to your boys. Same goes with developing empathy toward others.**

Reading this book is a good sign; you are obviously interested in helping your sons improve. But there is always more to learn. If you are open to new ideas, and learning how to incorporate those ideas into your existing knowledge of emotional regulation, empathy, teaching, and modeling, you will improve your ability to teach your boys valuable life lessons.[163]

As with the regulation question, test out this teaching tip with a real-life teacher. Find a good one, and ask if he or she has learned any new teaching strategies recently. Prepare to listen for a while.

> **TIP #061:** The more you learn about emotional regulation, empathy, and the teaching process, the better you will be at teaching this information to your boys. Keep learning; it will help!

5. **Help your boys believe they are the ones doing the hard work, not you.**

Sure, teachers have a difficult job—and in many ways they are responsible for whether or not their students succeed—but good teachers understand they are merely the catalyst for their students' improvement. They set the conditions and prime their

---

163 Strickland (2007)

students, but it is each individual student who is responsible for his or her success. The best teachers explain this to their students, and students respond with higher levels of motivation than students in learning environments where the teacher is taking all of the credit.[164]

Of course, you have a tremendous impact on how your sons turn out. But like a good teacher, you are only the catalyst. You have the ability to set the right conditions and steer your boys in the right direction. But you do not have control over what they do with your guidance. That is why it is important for you to explain to them that they are the ones who are doing the hard work—they are the ones who are responsible for learning how to grow into strong, powerful, respectful men. They are the ones who control their behavior and their understanding of others. You can help them along the way, but it is their responsibility.

> **TIP #062:** Students learn better when their teachers explain to them that their success is due to their own hard work—not the hard work of the teacher. Encourage your boys to believe that they are the ones doing the work—their motivation to continue to learn and change will increase as a result.[165]

6. Have your boys critique other people's emotional regulation and empathy abilities.

On the surface, this sounds like terrible advice. The last thing you want to do is pit your sons against each other or against their friends and family. And it seems as though encouraging them to critique others could lead to aggressiveness, power, and a feeling of superiority—the exact opposite of what you are attempting to teach them.

---

[164] Kozminsky & Kozminsky (2002)
[165] It has the added benefit of being true.

What good teachers know, however, is that boys learn well when they are required to provide their peers with feedback. Interestingly, the student who receives the feedback does not benefit much from that feedback. But the student who *gives* the feedback is forced to think critically about why the other student's assignment was a success or a failure. The *feedback-giver* is the one who ends up learning.[166]

This technique is similar to what I experienced during my 12-year tenure as a university professor.[167] I hope my students learned something from me, but thinking critically about the material and critiquing their work *forced me* to learn it very well.[168]

The key to adapting this technique to parenting is keeping the subject of the critique fairly abstract and distant. If you and your boys witness a person in public displaying terrible[169] emotional regulation or empathy skills, make a mental note to ask them to critique the stranger at a later time. Have your boys give you feedback about what that person did well, and what he could have done better. You can do the same thing with television, books, or movie characters.

A real-life example of this occurred for me a few days before writing this chapter. I was in line at a cable television service center,[170] waiting to pick up a new cable box. After about 20 minutes of waiting, an elderly man walked through the line and almost bumped into another man. In a fairly irritable tone, the aggrieved man said, "An *excuse me* would be nice." The elderly man's granddaughter then came over and explained that her grandfather was deaf and suffered from dementia. Rather than

---

[166] Li, et al. (2010)

[167] Technically, 11 years, 11 months.

[168] As a result, I am now super awesome.

[169] Or excellent—it is always good to focus on the positive.

[170] Second only to the DMV as a place that elicits frustration— in my opinion.

backing down, it appeared the younger man felt he needed to save face, so he doubled down on his angry responses. For about five minutes, he continued to rant—only halfway under his breath—about how he had been wronged. At first, I was very angry, but my anger quickly turned to embarrassment for him—he was so out of touch with his emotions that he had no idea how to react after making a mistake in public.

I didn't have my kids with me at the time. But if I had, this incident would have made for a great conversation in the car later in the day.

Here are some questions you can ask your boys to get them to effectively critique the (distant) individual:

6.a   What did he do well in that situation?

6.b   What did he do poorly?

6.c   How did others react to him?

6.d   Do you think he ended up getting what he wanted? Why or why not?

6.e   What do you think caused him to act the way he did?

6.f   What would you tell him to do differently next time?

6.g   If you had to grade him on a scale of A to F, what grade would you give him? Why?

> **TIP #063:** Have your boys critique other people's emotional regulation and empathy abilities (caveat: don't have them critique family members or close friends. Instead, have them critique strangers who you have just seen demonstrate good or bad emotional regulation or empathy—or have them critique television or movie characters).

7. **Engage your boys in active learning, not passive learning.**

Remember how bored you would get in school when you were sitting in your seat, listening to your teacher drone on and on and on?[171] Well, your boys remember that too. If you lecture them about how best to recognize and regulate their emotions, at some point they will tune you out. But if you teach them using an active learning approach, they will be much more receptive.[172]

Active learning is pretty much just what it sounds like. Rather than feeding your sons information in a passive way—such as in a lecture—ask them questions. Start a conversation. Get them to make connections. As the teacher, you guide the process, but your boys actively participate.

This is not a new approach to teaching. Socrates believed that everyone already had the answers they were looking for—they just needed a teacher to ask them the right questions so they could make the connections and necessary inferences to uncover their own knowledge.

Asking those Socratic questions is your job as a parent. Here is a list of examples:

7.a   Remember that woman who yelled in the grocery store? What do you think her irrational thought was?

7.b   What was it that caused you to get mad at your friend today?

7.c   Why so many temper tantrums this evening?

7.d   Remember when I was grouchy before dinner? What do you think was going through my mind?

7.e   Did you see that person talking to her friend? How do you think she knew what her friend was feeling?

---

[171] ... and on?
[172] Yoder & Hochevar (2005)

Notice, in each of the above examples, you are leading your boys somewhere. You are helping them actively engage in their learning, and you are guiding them through it. And remember, you can always correct your boys' answers if they are not quite right. That is part of teaching too.

> **TIP #064:** Active learning works better than passive learning. If you only lecture your boys, they will learn a little, but engaging them in conversations and asking them interesting questions will help them to learn, understand, and use the information you are teaching.

Here's one last caveat about engaging your boys in active learning: Use open-ended questions.

A close-ended question is one that your boys can answer quickly, requires little thought, and ends the discussion. They are typically framed in a yes/no manner. For example, "Did you have a good night's sleep?"

By contrast, an open-ended question is one that requires more thought and opens the door for reflection and ongoing conversation. This would be an example of an open-ended question: "How did you sleep last night?"

Keep in mind, if your boys are not in the mood to talk, they can answer most open-ended questions in a closed manner. For example, a response to the "How did you sleep last night" question could be "Fine." End of discussion.

In those cases, your boys might need a little more prompting to answer fully: "That's good. Tell me more about that," or, "What do you mean by fine? Help me understand what that means for you." When your boys try to shut it down, you can also comment on the *process* of the discussion: "It seems like you aren't in the mood to talk about it right now. Why not?"

In many cases, when your boys are answering questions in a brief, closed manner, it just means it is not the right time to teach them anything. Let them go be kids for a while and try again later. If they shut you down *every time* you try to bring it up, you might need professional help.

> **TIP #065:** Ask your boys open-ended questions to push them to think harder about their answers and to foster the conversation.

> **TIP #066:** If your boys are shutting down the lines of communication as you are asking them questions, give them a break and try again later.

> **TIP #067:** If your boys are not listening to you at all—and shutting you down every time you try to engage with them—you might want to consider family counseling to get the ball rolling.

8. **Give your boys a quiz every now and then.**

Oh, the horror of the pop quiz. Students *hate* them. They raise anxiety. They feel cruel. Yet good teachers know that periodic (and brief) quizzes help students learn and remember information.[173] Terrorizing students with incredibly difficult, surprise tests is unnecessary, but short quizzes every now and then do wonders for learning.

As a parent, you have to be careful with this teaching technique—you do not want your sons to think you are insane. Don't have them sit down and take a written quiz.[174] Instead, present them with an emotional situation and have a few Socratic-style questions prepared to ask them about it. Don't call it a quiz, though. Instead, let them know you want to see how much they have learned about reflection, automatic thoughts, emotional

---

[173] Agarwal, et al. (2012)

[174] Depending on their age, a written quiz might not be possible. No matter their age, though, it is a really bad idea.

regulation, empathy, and the like. The slight pressure of being quizzed[175] will help them retain the information you are teaching.

> **TIP #068:** Give your boys a quiz. Ask your boys every now and then to help you analyze an emotional situation, to make sure they have understood your teaching.

> **TIP #069:** Don't go overboard on the quizzing. Your boys will quickly start to resent you, and you will end up contributing to a future therapist's house payment.[176]

9. Provide feedback to your sons as quickly as possible.

Don't wait too long to start giving feedback to your sons about how they are doing. The sooner you let them know what they are doing right and what they are doing wrong, the more they will learn. Teachers who provide feedback to students quickly have students who learn fundamental skills better.[177]

There is a catch, of course. It is very important that you avoid being too negative or harsh when your sons get it wrong. Keep in mind they are learning, and they are not going to do everything correctly the first time around. By being too harsh, you can actually discourage your boys from trying harder next time.

Here is a list of tips for providing feedback your sons will be able to hear:

9.a Always emphasize the positive: Make sure you tell your sons what they did right before you explain to them what they did wrong.

---

[175] ... even though you aren't calling it a quiz.
[176] If future therapy is necessary, my contact information is readily available online.
[177] Chen, et al. (2010)

9.b   If they didn't do anything right, emphasize that you see how hard they are trying and tell them that with a few changes, you know they are going to improve.

9.c   Don't tell your boys they did things *wrong*. Instead, describe the areas where they made mistakes.

9.d   Remind them that they *know* how to do it correctly. If they have done it correctly in the past, remind them of their successes.

9.e   Tell them you know they are going to do better next time, because you see them trying hard.

> **TIP #070:** The sooner you can provide kind feedback to your boys on how they are doing with regard to emotional regulation and empathy skills, the better they will be at fixing their mistakes.

10.   **Continuously work on developing a positive relationship between you and your boys.**

Teachers who work to build positive relationships with their students have students who learn more information.[178] In fact, *this tip is so important that, even if you ignore every other tip in the book and only follow this one, you will probably raise decent boys.* If they have a stable parental relationship,[179] they will develop in positive ways.

Here are some tips to help you foster your relationship with your boys:

10.a   Be nice to them.

---

178 Lenz, et al. (2003)

179 Or stable relationships with multiple parental figures, whether those people are aunts, uncles, adoptive parents, grandparents, or guardians.

10.b Set firm but reasonable limits.

10.c Explain to them why you have set limits. Even very
young boys can benefit from hearing an explanation.
"Because I said so" is a recipe for disaster. Here is an
example: You want your son to go to bed, but he wants
to stay up and play. When he asks you why he can't
stay awake, you could respond with, "Because I said
so," or you could respond with, "Because you have to
get up for school tomorrow morning and you will be
exhausted if you don't get enough sleep. Remember
how miserable you feel when you are tired?" Now,
which of these explanations would *you* rather hear?
Even if your son reacts to the full and thorough
explanation in a negative way, like throwing a temper
tantrum, at least he knows you have a reason for telling
him to go to bed. If he hears your reasoning over and
over again, it will sink in that you are not just telling
him to do certain things because you said so.

10.d If you cannot think of a good reason why you are
setting a particular limit beyond "Because I said so,"
or "Because it is good for you," it might not be a necessary limit. It is okay to back down from these limits
every now and then. When your son asks you, "Why
do I have to clean my room before I call my friend?"
and you realize that your only reply is, "Because I said
so," you should rethink whether it is really a necessary
limit. If you realize that it is *not* that important, you
can always say, "Well, I'm not sure why you need to do
that. I guess it is okay for you to call your friend first,
as long as you clean your room today."

10.e Let them know you are there to protect them and keep
them safe.

10.f Listen to them.

10.g Tell them you are willing to hear whatever they have to say. You will sometimes need to punish them because of what they tell you, but you should *always, always, always* praise them for telling you the truth.

TIP #071: Work on your relationship with your boys! They will benefit in numerous ways, and they will be much more willing to learn from you.

TIP #072: Always praise your boys for telling you the truth, even if you have to then mete out a punishment. They should never feel like they are getting in trouble because they talked to you.

Summary: five bonus tips for teaching your boys

Following the steps in Chapter 4 will help you understand how to recognize and control emotions and how to have empathy for others. It will give you a good idea of what your boys will need to learn to do the same. However, sharing that information with your boys in a way that maximizes their ability to learn can be tricky. The ten tips mentioned in this chapter are a great place to start. They will help you teach your boys how to master the techniques in this book in order to develop into strong individuals.

You should consider the steps in this chapter to be good guidelines for effective teaching, but it is not necessary to utilize all of them as you are raising your sons. In fact, that would be impossible. With that in mind, it can help to take just a few of the tips to heart and use them as you work with your sons, helping them learn to recognize and control their emotions. Pick two or three that resonate with you and seem easy to implement, and then go for it.

And if those ten teaching tips weren't enough for you, there are a number of other simple steps you can take to make the most of your ability to teach your sons.

Here are five quick ones:

1. Be open to the idea of change.

2. Understand your own 'stuff' and don't let it get in your way.

3. Don't overwhelm your boys with too much at once. Infuse your teaching into everyday conversations a little bit at a time.

4. Always be on the lookout for a teaching moment.

5. Know that your boys will make mistakes.

1. **Be open to the idea of change.**

It is important for you to be ready to make a change in the way you raise your sons. For some of you who are reading this book, the changes I am asking you to make are small. For others, these changes may represent a fundamental shift in the way you think of masculinity. If you aren't ready to make that shift, the tips and instructions in this book won't work for you or your family. That is okay.

But you must be realistic about it. How ready are you to make a change—small or large?

Here is a list of questions you can ask yourself to see how ready you are to make this change:

1.a Are you excited about the change?

1.b Are you reading this book because you thought it was a good idea, or did someone else tell you to read it?

1.c What are the benefits of changing?

1.d What are the drawbacks to changing?

1.e When do you want to make the change? Immediately? Later? Never?

There are two issues that are important to keep in mind when thinking about readiness for change. First, people typically do not make a lasting change until the drawbacks of the current behavior outweigh the benefits.[180] For example, a smoker will not quit smoking until the negative effects of smoking outweigh the positive effects.[181]

Second, just because you decide you're not ready to change right now, that does not mean you will never be ready to change. If you aren't ready yet, reassess yourself in a few months or a year. Maybe the time will be right then.

> **TIP #073:** Assess how ready you are to make some major changes in your parenting style. If you are highly motivated to do it right away, great! If not, that is okay too. But don't expect big things to happen if you are not ready to work hard to make changes. Instead, reassess yourself at a later date—weigh the pros and cons of changing and see if you are ready.

> **TIP #074:** You also need to determine if all of the parental figures in the household are ready to make a change. If not, it will make your job considerably more challenging.

2. **Understand your own 'stuff' and don't let it get in your way.**

---

180 Connors, et al. (2013)
181 Although it may not be healthy, many people gain numerous 'benefits' from smoking. Otherwise, they wouldn't do it.

I don't need to emphasize this any more than I already have—other than to say that the exercises in Chapter 4 will minimize the interference of your baggage on your ability to teach your boys. The more you get a handle on your own emotions, the more convincing you will be with your sons.

> **TIP #075:** Be aware of your own baggage and try to keep it from getting in your way.

3. Don't overwhelm your boys with too much at once. Infuse your teaching into everyday conversations a little bit at a time.

Your boys will become completely overwhelmed if you hit them with too much information all at once, and they will get sick of you talking about it all the time. Remember, you do not need to solve this problem completely in one day. It will take time. Pace yourself. Find some ways to organically infuse your teaching into everyday conversations, and give your boys a break.

> **TIP #076:** You need to assess your readiness for change, but you also need to assess how ready your boys are. If you hit them with too much at once, it will be very difficult for them to learn anything. Take it slowly at first and gauge how well they are responding.

4. Always be on the lookout for a teaching moment.

Didn't I just say not to do this? Not exactly. Yes, your boys will get sick of it if you are talking about emotions all of the time. That is why it's important to make the conversations you do have seem as natural as possible. At times, you might want to set aside certain portions of the day to specifically work on these issues. But it will be more meaningful to your boys if you look for natural opportunities to discuss emotional regulation strategies. This works for boys of all ages, even preschoolers.[182] In fact, it can even help your preschooler's cognitive development.[183] When you see a person flip out in public, you can have a quick discussion about it on your drive home. If your son gets in trouble in school, take some time before bed to help him reflect on his emotional experience and think of how he might like to react differently next time.

> **TIP #077:** Look for natural ways to bring your teaching into your everyday life with your boys. Don't force it.

5. Know that your boys will make mistakes.

What more needs to be said about this one? No one is perfect. There is a major difference between your boy making a mistake and your boy being a psychopath. Just because he makes a mistake, it does not mean he is starting over from square one. Your teaching will sink in, and most of the time, he will get it.

Every now and then, he'll screw up. *And that is okay.* Help him learn from his mistake, and try not to be too hard on him.

> **TIP #078:** Your boys will make mistakes sometimes. Be okay with that.

However, if your boy is constantly making mistakes and seems truly unable to control his emotions or understand others' emotional experiences, you may need to solicit professional help.

> **TIP #079:** Be open to the idea of professional help if it seems warranted. The techniques in this book will not work perfectly. But if they don't work at all, there may be a problem that a professional can help you address.

---

[182] Callanan & Braswell (2006); Carr (2011)
[183] Slaughter & Peterson (2012)

CHAPTER 6

Tying It All Together: what
to do and what to say

At this point, I have covered a lot of information. The previous five chapters contain the information you will need to teach your boys how to reflect on their experiences, recognize their emotions, and control their behavior. These skills are the building blocks for empathy, which you have also learned is one of the main traits you want your boys to develop in order to become responsible men. It will help them fully experience their humanity, and it will help them improve the world.

This chapter summarizes the steps required to teach your boys properly, and it will provide you with an action plan to put into place in order to maximize your effectiveness.

As a reminder, here are the steps to get your boys to understand and recognize their emotions and be empathic toward others through reflective thinking:

1. Understand your own emotions first.

2. Regulate your own emotions.

3. Model the behavior you want your boys to exhibit.

4. Teach your boys how to understand and regulate their emotions.

5. Teach your boys how to have empathy for others.

That's it. It is very simple. In fact, why are there five chapters preceding this one? A pamphlet would have sufficed.

I suppose the answer to that question is that, although it sounds very simple, it is easier said (or read) than done. What I am asking you to do is contemplate changing how you raise your boys. For some of you, it will only take minor tweaking. For others, this will be a fundamental shift in what you have been doing and how you have been taught to raise boys. It is going to take time, effort, and a willingness to make mistakes. You will also have to be okay with short-term strife—if you are having a hard time with these changes, it is reasonable to assume your boys will have some difficulty too.

In order to help you organize your thoughts and put the advice in this book into practice, I will go through each of the steps above and list specific actions you can take, questions you can ask yourself, and teaching techniques you can use. Basically, I will provide an outline summary you can quickly use as a reference. I will skip the explanations that accompany each of the outlined points, and if you need more information about that particular topic, you can find it earlier in the book.

SUMMARY OUTLINE

1. <u>Understand your own emotions first.</u>

    A.   Identify the emotion you are experiencing.

        1.   Say to yourself (or write down[184]), "I feel _____."

    B.   Identify the most immediate cause of that emotion.

        2.   Say to yourself (or write down), "I feel _____ because _____."

    C.   Think about why you experienced the emotion you are feeling, as opposed to other potential emotional reactions.

        1.   Find a list of emotion words on the internet.

        2.   Examine that list and determine which other emotions might have been reasonable to experience in addition to, or instead of, your current emotion.

---

[184] It is not always possible to do this, but if you have time, writing out your answers is extremely helpful.

2. Regulate your emotions.

    A.   Identify the additional factors (aside from the immediate cause) that led you to feel your current emotion.

        1.   Think about (or write down) how your day went.

        2.   List the day's activities that could have added to your stress, anger, sadness, happiness, etc.

    B.   Dispute those other factors and make a positive emotional change.

        1.   For each additional factor, think about (or write down) the thought that explains why it is contributing to your current mood. (e.g. You are running late, and your belief about running late is that people will be angry with you if you do not get there on time.)

        2.   Think about whether that thought/belief is rational. (Isn't it possible that people will be understanding if you are late, because everyone is late sometimes?)

        3.   If it is not a rational thought, dispute it and change it. (e.g. *Tell yourself,* "Everyone is late sometimes, and it is not going to be a big deal. I am going to choose to calm down about it, because stressing out is not going to make traffic move any faster.")

        4.   If it is a rational thought leading to a rational but negative emotion (such as extreme sadness when a loved one dies, because your thought is that it is a tragedy when someone passes

away), learn ways to cope with those emotions *so they do not turn into bad behaviors.*

3. <u>Model the behavior you want your boys to exhibit.</u>

    A.   Make sure your boys witness you *understanding* your emotions.

        1.   This will require some explanation from you, as they are not going to be able to read your mind. *Tell them* how you determined what your emotions were and why you were feeling that way.

    B.   Make sure your boys see you *regulating* your emotions

        1.   Some of this will be visible to them. (e.g. They will see you reacting in a positive way rather than throwing a hissy fit in stop-and-go traffic.)

        2.   You will need to explain some of this process to them. (Tell them how you determined you were in a bad mood because you were running late and how you disputed the irrational thought and the belief behind it.)

4. <u>Teach your boys how to understand and regulate their emotions.</u>

    A.   Follow the steps in the above outline, detailed in Chapter 4, to teach your boys what you have learned to do.

    B.   Use some of the specific techniques covered in Chapter 5 to bolster your teaching ability. In an ideal world, you might use all of the tips mentioned in that chapter, but you should be realistic with yourself—that is impossible. Just pick the few that make the most sense for you and your boys. As you get better, you can incorporate more of the Chapter 5 strategies into your teaching. Here is the list from Chapter 5:

a. Reflect on your teaching skills.

b. Give yourself the freedom to try new parenting techniques.

c. Help your sons take responsibility for their learning.

d. Keep learning new parenting/teaching skills.

e. Help your boys understand that they are the ones doing the hard work.

f. Have your boys critique others.

g. Engage your boys in active learning.

h. Give your boys a quiz every now and then.

i. Provide feedback to your sons quickly.

j. Continue to work on developing a positive relationship with your boys.

k. Be open to the idea of change.

l. Understand your own stuff and don't let it get in your way.

m. Don't overwhelm your boys with too much all at once.

n. Always be on the lookout for natural teaching moments.

o. Be okay with your boys making mistakes.

5. <u>Teach your boys how to have empathy for others.</u>

A. A. Follow the same steps mentioned above and in Chapter 4. Instead of applying the techniques to themselves, have your boys apply those techniques to other people, in order to better understand where they are coming from.

B. Use some of the teaching techniques from Chapter 5, outlined above.

SAMPLE QUESTIONS
AND STATEMENTS

One of the most difficult aspects of teaching your boys how to recognize and regulate their emotions and have empathy toward others is figuring out exactly what to say to them to get them to learn. Chapters 3, 4, and 5 give you some structure in terms of the overall teaching process, but I thought it would be helpful to include a concrete list of questions and statements to help you get started. There is nothing particularly magical about these phrases. If you come up with statements on your own that work, great. The statements in this chapter will just point you in the right direction if you are having trouble getting started.

The questions and statements listed here are phrased as if you were talking directly to one of your sons. They can be easily adapted to other situations. For example, you can use them to ask yourself questions about how you are feeling ... or you can change them to ask questions of your boys about a television character who has just behaved badly.[185]

1. <u>Teaching your son to understand his and others' emotions.</u>

    A.   How are you feeling right now?

---

[185] Or who has just behaved well. Remember to focus on the positive!

B. How were you feeling when _____ happened? (e.g. How were you feeling when *that other boy kicked you in the crotch?*)

C. How were you feeling when you did _____? (e.g. How were you feeling when *you set fire to the neighbor's mailbox?*)

D. What are you thinking right now? (Sometimes this is a good place to start, and then you can ask follow-up questions about feelings.)

E. What were you thinking about when _____ happened?

F. What were you thinking when you did _____?

G. Are you feeling sad/angry/happy/frustrated/per-plexed/etc.? (Sometimes you will need to give your son a few options before he can identify his emotion.)

H. Go through an emotion word list with your son and help him pick out the emotion(s) he is feeling

I. Why are you/were you feeling _____?

J. Why did you _____ when you were feeling _____? (e.g. Why did you *run over your sister's Barbies with your bike* when you were feeling *vexed?*)

K. Are you proud of the way you handled yourself when you were feeling _____? Why? Why not? (e.g. Are you proud of *biting the babysitter* because you were *mad that she ate the last Oreo?* Why not?)

L. So, you feel _____ because _____? (e.g. So, you feel *sad* because *you flushed your favorite Lego down the toilet?*)

SPECIAL NOTE: This last statement is the most important question/statement you can make to your son in terms of helping him to understand his emotions. The ultimate goal is to get him to start saying this to you spontaneously. If he can say *what* he is feeling and *why* he is feeling it, he is on his way to understanding his emotions, regulating his feelings and behavior, and having empathy toward others.

2. Teaching your son to regulate his emotions.

    A.   What has been going on today that could have caused you to feel _____?

    B.   How has your day been going?

    C.   Let's talk about how your day has been going. (Then help your son list the day's events.)

    D.   Do you think you feel _____ now because _____? (e.g. Do you think you feel *angry* now *because you skipped lunch?* or Do you think you feel *sad* now *because you threw up on your stuffed animal yesterday*? Sometimes it can be helpful to give your son some concrete suggestions—especially if he is having a hard time thinking of how previous events could be affecting his current mood. This is part of the Socratic method.)

    E.   What other emotions could you have felt instead of _____?

    F.   Do you think everyone would have felt that way if _____ happened? Why? Why not?

    G.   Why did you feel _____ instead of _____? (e.g. Why did you feel *sad* instead of *angry*?)

H. What do you think caused you to feel _____ instead of _____?

I. What is the thought behind your emotion?

J. What is your belief about _____ that caused you to feel _____? (e.g. What is your belief about *your sister farting on your head* that caused you to feel *enraged*?)

K. Sometimes, when I feel _____ about _____, it's because I think _____. I have to remind myself, that that's not always the case. What do you think? (e.g. Sometimes, when I *get angry* about *losing something*, it's *because I think it's going to be impossible to replace. I have to remind myself that some things are easy to replace and some are not. Do you think that piece of garbage you've been carrying around for the past three days would be easy or hard to replace?*)

L. Do you think _____ is a rational thought? Why? Why not?

M. Does thinking _____ in this situation make sense? Why? Why Not?

N. How do you think you could dispute the thought that doesn't make sense?

O. If the same thing happened to your friend and you tried to explain to him why his thinking doesn't make sense, what would you say?

P. What are some ways you could change your thinking so that it makes more sense?

Q. When that happened to me, I thought _____, and it helped. (e.g. When *my brother told me my parents hated me,* I thought *that can't possibly be true. They show me their love every day.* That helped me *calm down enough that I didn't want to throw him down the stairs anymore.*)

R. You know, I think you might be right. What you're thinking makes sense, and it seems normal to feel _____ about it. But that doesn't mean you can behave badly. What else do you think you could do?

S. It's okay to feel _____, but it's not okay to act the way you're acting.

T. Do you think the way you're acting is going to make things better or worse?

U. What could you do to make things better?

V. The next time you're right for feeling _____, maybe you could try _____. How do you think that could help? (e.g. The next time you are right for feeling *angry because that bully hit your friend,* maybe you could *immediately tell a grown up to make sure it does not happen to you or any of your friends again.* How do you think that would work, *as opposed to what you actually did, which was give him an atomic wedgie?*)

W. When I am thinking rationally and feeling _____, I remind myself that it is painful now, but I am strong enough to deal with it without hurting others. That helps me. (e.g. When I am thinking rationally and feeling *angry for a good reason,* I remind myself that *it is hard to feel this angry and not act out, but I am strong enough to keep from doing or saying anything that will hurt other people.* That helps me.

SPECIAL NOTE: This last statement is another key to raising healthy boys. By teaching your boys to believe, "This is hard, but I can handle it," you are giving them the strength to regulate their emotions and deal with negative emotions in a positive way. Anyone can start a war—it takes real strength to resolve differences peacefully.

CHAPTER 7

*But It Isn't Working: what to do
when you run into difficulties*

I have covered the theory behind my suggestions, and I have offered myriad tips on how to implement those suggestions. It *should* work. It *should* help. And in most cases, it will. Both you and your boys will benefit greatly from learning reflective-thinking techniques. Your family will see a dramatic change in your sons' ability to understand their own emotions, understand the feelings of others, and regulate their emotional and behavioral reactions. For most of you, it will be great. You will prepare your boys for a life filled with strong leadership, good friends, and responsible success.

But it won't work perfectly for everyone. Even in cases where it does work well, it won't work all of the time. In some extreme cases, it won't work at all.

That is where this chapter fits into the larger picture. I will cover a number of the most common scenarios that can derail the processes described in earlier chapters, and I will give some tips on how to overcome those issues.

A major issue for everyone: it is taking too long

Don't expect to see permanent changes in your child immediately. Behavior change takes patience on the part of the parent and the child, and it can sometimes be a frustrating process. For most boys, you will probably see some subtle changes fairly quickly (within a few days or a week of using the techniques in this book). But, you will also see your boy continuing to make mistakes and having problems putting these skills into action. In some cases, you might even notice your boy's behavior getting worse—this is a common, temporary phenomenon when attempting to change someone's behavior.

Give it a little time. If you are consistent with this book's recommendations, you should start seeing changes in your child within a few weeks, and the temporary worsening of behavior should go away. Within a few months of consistent practice, you should see noticeable improvement in your boy's ability to understand and regulate his emotions better and to have empathy for others. And, this is a life-long process—he will continue to get better at it over time, and he will continue to make mistakes every now and then.

Maybe my son is just a bad seed

If you have ever wondered if your child is Rosemary's Baby,[186] you are not alone. A normal part of human development, especially at young ages, mimics pure evil. For example, it is normal for young children to be self-centered and narcissistic as a way of developing

---

186 If you don't get this reference, put this book down immediately and watch Rosemary's Baby, the 1968 film starring Mia Farrow. I won't spoil it for you, but let's just say Rosemary has a child who is a bit on the evil side.

a healthy self-esteem.[187] In fact, some theorists believe that both young boys and teenagers *use* narcissism and a feeling of being all-powerful to help them learn how to reconcile how they would like to be with how they actually are[188]—in other words, they truly believe they are strong enough to become better people.

In addition to egocentricity and thinking that they are the most important people on earth, your young sons will display a lot of other symptoms that, in an adult, would constitute a serious personality disorder. As they are learning to separate themselves from their parents, they will experience an all-or-nothing, push-pull attitude. In one moment, they will push their parents away ("I can do it on my own!"), and in the next moment, they will run to their parents, screaming for help and reassurance. This phenomenon is known as *rapprochement*, and it is perfectly normal in young boys.[189] In adults, however, it is referred to as Borderline Personality Disorder. So ... it is definitely possible that your little ones may be temporarily evil. The key word in that last sentence, though, is *temporarily*. In most cases, normal parenting helps boys work through these difficult stages and develop into normal humans. The strategies in this book can certainly help.

Unfortunately, it is also possible that some boys might be genetically predisposed toward anger, impulsivity, behavioral problems, and antisocial emotions. Researchers are discovering genetic and biological anomalies that are linked to some bad behaviors. For example, a study from 2013 found that certain genetic markers in kids are related to negative emotions, impulsivity, and irresponsibility. These particular researchers were able to conclude that childhood abuse, or the lack thereof, did not make a difference in predicting whether the children with these markers developed antisocial traits. Regardless of how good or bad their home environment was, a lot of the kids with these

[187] Boekholt & des Ligneris (2003)
[188] Bleiberg (1988)
[189] Mahler, et al. (1994)

genetic markers developed some antisocial tendencies.[190] (And, in case you are thinking this is just an isolated finding, other researchers have reached similar conclusions.[191])

With this research in mind, it is certainly worth entertaining the notion that some boys are born to be bad. But it is also important to note that, although the study mentioned above found that negative home environment had no effect on the development of antisocial tendencies, most of the current research is clear that *genetics are not destiny.*[192] It is quite likely that fostering a positive environment can keep boys who possess the genetic and biological markers for antisocial behavior from turning into psychopaths. In fact, these studies all have strong findings explaining that genetics cause about 40-50% of kids' psychopathic and antisocial tendencies. The child's environment causes the rest. And that is also true of most major mental illnesses, including Major Depression[193], Bipolar Disorder[194], and Generalized Anxiety Disorder.[195]

So although it is certainly possible that you have a bad seed who is beyond hope no matter what, that is *extremely* rare. You might have a boy who has to work a little harder to be good, just like you might have a boy who needs to work a little harder to keep from being sad or anxious. But there are good, positive steps you can take to improve your son's life. And for those of you who are in the extreme minority and have a boy who seems to do everything wrong, no matter what you try, it is important for you to seek professional help. The sooner the better.[196]

---

[190] Sadeh, et al. (2013)

[191] Pemment (2013); Raine (2013); Schlitz, et al. (2011)

[192] Beaver, et al. (2011); Bezdijian, et al. (2011); Hicks, et al. (2012); Vidding & McCrory (2012)

[193] Benjamin & Taylor (2010)

[194] Cho, et al. (2005)

[195] Hettema, et al. (2001)

[196] In many states, the legal age to consent to psychotherapeutic treatment without a parent's permission is 15. That means

TIP #080: The vast majority of boys will respond well to positive environments, even the ones with a genetic predisposition for badness.

TIP #081: There will be a small minority of boys who do not respond to the techniques in this book or any other positive changes you try to make in their lives. In those cases, it is extremely important for you to get professional help to determine what is happening and how to work through it. That is what the experts are there for.

My son is in a rebellious phase and won't listen to anything I tell him

There was a classic study, conducted in 1959, examining rebellion in children.[197] In this study, the kids who had severe discipline problems and ignored their parents' wishes were found to have *unrealistic self-regard*.[198] They also thought they were better than their parents. By contrast, the kids in the study who did *not* have discipline problems and did not display rebellious behavior had reasonable levels of self-regard and admired their parents.[199]

In case you're thinking that the world of rebellious teenagers has changed since the 1950s,[200] you should think again. When it comes to child rebelliousness, little has changed. As recently as 2008, researchers confirmed that a healthy respect for parental

---

a 15-year-old boy can also refuse to participate in psychotherapy, and the parents can't legally do anything about it.

[197] In my mind, I picture the characters from *Grease* being part of this study.

[198] In other words, they thought they were really awesome.

[199] Shippee-Blum (1959)

[200] Come on, I know you're picturing John Travolta and Olivia Newton John right now.

authority was the key to determining whether a child would be rebellious or not. In fact, higher levels of appropriate discipline and good parental communication seem to be the best ways to curb rebelliousness.[201]

> **TIP #082:** Appropriate discipline in the face of rebelliousness can curb this problem in your boys. Set firm but reasonable limits and explain why they are in trouble. "Because I said so" is one of the worst things you can say to your boys. "So that you'll learn" is probably just as bad. For example: "Mom, why did you ground me for a month?" "So you'll learn to behave!" A month's worth of grounding is only going to teach your son how to sneak things by you. If you can't explain to yourself why you are setting the limit you are setting, it is probably an unreasonable one.

> **TIP #083:** Communicate with your boys. Tell them what you are doing. Tell them why you are doing it. Tell them why their behavior is wrong. Explain the potential consequences of bad behavior. Listen to their side of the story. Let them complain. Talk with them. Allow them to raise their concerns, especially if they are expressing their negative emotions appropriately. They may not be happy about the outcome, but they will respect you more for it.

It is also important to remember that certain types of rebelliousness can be perfectly normal for boys. Remember the phenomenon of *rapprochement*? Children learn to become autonomous people by alternating between pushing their parents away

---

[201] Dixon, et al. (2008)

and then running back to them for comfort. In the teen years, this is a big part of what normal rebelliousness is about.

And it's important to tolerate a certain amount of rebelliousness in your boys. Most of the time, the disobedience you experience from your sons is transient—a phase they are going through. Or maybe they're having a bad day. Or maybe they're tired. As long as they aren't being overly disrespectful, acting out, or doing anything dangerous, some short-lived rebellion is okay.

There is a common theory that when a boy acts out or disobeys his parents, it is because he wants their attention. Even negative attention is better than no attention. This theory makes a lot of sense. But it does not seem to be true. What appears to be more important in predicting rebelliousness and rebellious behaviors in boys are negative emotions and high levels of strife in the family.[202] If the parents are jerks, they are probably going to raise boys who are jerks too. Conversely, if you are able to provide a loving, stable environment for your boys, their level of rebelliousness will lower and they will be more likely to grow into mature, healthy men. The rebelliousness they exhibit will not be about gaining your attention. In fact, your attention may be an unintended and unpleasant outcome for them. Instead, it will be about learning healthy boundaries in order to develop into autonomous, well-adjusted adults.

> **TIP #084:** Lower the level of negative emotions (anger, anxiety, depression) in the home. It will reduce the chances of your boys becoming overly rebellious. Keep in mind if someone in the home is depressed or anxious, he or she might need professional help.

> **TIP #085:** Lower the level of family discord in order to reduce the chances your boys will

---

[202] Bornovalova, et al. (2012); Harvey, et al. (2011); Singh & Waldman (2010)

become rebellious. This does not mean you have
to be perfect, but, if you and your partner are
constantly arguing, figure out how to stop.

It is important to distinguish normal disobedience from problematic rebelliousness. Normal disobedience is temporary, and
it is typically explained by the changing circumstances in your
sons' lives. If your boys are acting out for a few days, or a few
weeks, or even a few months, it does not mean they are doomed
to a life filled with disaster and strife. Think about what is going
on in their lives. Are they going through a new developmental
milestone? Is something stressful happening at school? Did they
have a falling out with a friend? Did a loved one pass away? These
situational stressors can all be triggers for short-lived, normal
periods of rebelliousness.

In these cases, you just need to ride out the storm. With some
loving patience on your part, along with guidance for your boys
so they understand why they're in such a bad mood, you can be
reasonably assured that your sweet little angels will return soon.
You also need to let them know that expressing their emotions is
okay, but acting dangerously is not.

However, it is crucial to determine when a boy's rebelliousness
is more than just a temporary phenomenon—when it is a consistent issue being caused by negative emotions in the home, family
discord, or the child's temperament. Along with negative emotions and family discord, one of the best predictors of whether or
not present rebelliousness is going to be problematic in the future
is to examine the level of *agreeableness* of your boy. In a study
conducted over a period of 25 years, researchers determined that
8-year-old boys who had significant problems with aggressiveness, disobedience, and self-control turned into adults who were
low on the *agreeableness* personality factor. These adults had
more problems with alcoholism, depression, job instability, and

illegal activity. It also turned out that those low-agreeable adults were also low-agreeable boys.[203]

To most people, *agreeableness* sounds like compliance. An agreeable boy is willing to do what others tell him. While compliance is a part of agreeableness, there is more to it than that. Boys who are agreeable tend to be trusting, view others as honest, and express empathy. They will be more willing to help other people, and they avoid manipulation. Here is a list of questions you can ask yourself to determine how agreeable your boy is. A *Yes* or a *No* in parentheses after the question indicates the answer that points toward agreeableness:

1. Does he trust other people? (Yes)

2. Most of the time, does he obey authority figures? (Yes)

3. Is he suspicious of others' motives? (No)

4. Is he empathic? (Yes)

5. Does he like to compete more than he likes cooperation? (No)

6. Does he like to help others? (Yes)

7. Is he manipulative with his friends? (No)

8. Is he modest? (Yes)

9. Is he tender-minded, or a little sweetheart? (Yes)

Please keep in mind this is not a scientific test. It is not possible to diagnose anyone with any type of mental condition using these questions, and there is no magic number (like 5 out of 9, for example) to determine if your boy is agreeable or not. But it should be helpful enough to give you a framework to start understanding this facet of his personality. The more agreeable he is,

---

[203] Laursen, et al. (2002)

the more likely his rebelliousness is a phase that he will move through with little permanent damage.

> **TIP #086:** Use the nine questions above to think about your boys' personalities. If they are displaying rebelliousness but seem to be fairly agreeable, their rebelliousness is most likely not problematic. If they seem to be more on the low-agreeableness end, you might want to consider some professional help from a family therapist— someone who can help you learn to communicate and discipline in an appropriate way in order to curb the rebelliousness before it becomes a life-long issue.

It seemed to be going well, but my son just made a big mistake

This is a frustrating one. It seems like the hours, days, years of hard work are paying off and we are feeling great about our parenting ability. We have read a ton of books, we have consulted experts, and we have raised our boys with empathy and compassion. And then, we get a call from the principal saying they just set fire to a school bathroom.

Before I address this issue directly, let me tell a story from my childhood. In the small town where I grew up, our elementary schools went through the sixth grade, and we did not have middle schools. We had a junior high school for seventh and eighth graders, and then we went to high school.

If any of you remember seventh grade, you will vaguely recall it being horrible. The popular kids were miserable because they were afraid they would no longer be popular if they did something stupid. The unpopular kids were miserable because they weren't popular. There was a lot of acne. Voices cracked. Things started poking out uncontrollably. Horrible.

I was a sweet, naive kid in elementary school. For some reason, I was oblivious to the social drama that other kids seemed to be facing in fifth and sixth grade. All I thought about was baseball and toys. I was off the charts on the agreeableness scale.

Needless to say, seventh grade hit me like a ton of bricks. Kids cared about their clothes? There was more than one way to cut your hair? People don't do everything their teachers or parents tell them to do?

It was a huge culture shock for me, but I adjusted quickly, changing from a sweet child to a terrified, angry preteen—just like everyone else—in a matter of weeks. And that is when I got into my first, and only, fight.

I still remember it clearly. This one other boy and I had been eyeing each other for a few days, giving one another dirty looks and purposefully bumping into each other in the hallways. I have absolutely no idea why I was mad at him. Even as an adult, I have no clue. He probably didn't know either.

But we rode home on the same bus, and on Thursday, I decided to sit in the seat right in front of him. We exchanged unpleasantries as I sat down, and we continued to needle each other for the next fifteen minutes. Eventually, I said something to him that pushed him over the edge, and he stood up, leaned forward, and put me in a headlock. Spastically, I swung my arm behind me, and the side of my hand made contact with his nose.

He immediately let go of me, and I turned to see that his nose was bleeding. Each of us remained in our seats for the rest of the bus ride, and we didn't say a word to each other.

When I got home, I burst into tears and told my parents what happened. I looked up his phone number[204] and called him to

---

[204] As an aside, our phone numbers back then only had five digits. My number was 2-7876.

apologize. I don't think I talked to him ever again. That was also the last time I ever hit anyone on purpose.

Here is the point of the story: Your boys will mess up. They are not perfect—no one is. Plus, they are going through all kinds of developmental changes that affect them dramatically, both physically and mentally. It is okay to cut them a little slack.

The key is to help your boys reflect on their mistakes. At first, they will need help with this task. Ideally, they will learn to do it on their own. Talk with them about how no one is good all of the time and that everyone will make mistakes. Use the techniques in Chapters 4 and 5 (and the sample questions from Chapter 6) to get them to understand how to behave differently next time. Also, remind them that you are proud of them for being able to talk to you about what happened. Mete out the appropriate punishment,[205] and explain to them that you know they have learned their lesson.

The key is to communicate and use effective discipline. The best way to keep a one-time mistake from becoming a common occurrence is to help your boys to learn from their missteps and to show them they can talk to you about anything. This works for boys from preschool through adolescence,[206] although adolescents will tend to share less and less with their parents over time.[207] That, however, is a normal part of growing up too.

By the way, if you are tempted to snoop through your boys' stuff to determine whether they are behaving, that is a guarantee that they will stop sharing information with you. You will actually end up knowing less about your boys if you try to snoop on them.[208]

---

[205] If punishment is necessary. Not every mistake will require discipline.

[206] Edwards, et al. (2010); Klahr, et al. (2011); Wilson, et al. (2012)

[207] Keijsers & Poulin (2013)

[208] Hawk, et al. (2009); Hawk, et al. (2013).

TIP #087: If you want your boys to talk to you, do not snoop on them. Invading their privacy will cause them to shut down the lines of communication, and you will end up knowing less about them than if you did not snoop.

Here is a good set of steps to follow when your boys mess up:

1. Don't panic. No one is perfect. Every boy will do stupid things periodically.

2. Explain you are proud of them for talking to you about the problem instead of trying to hide it from you.

3. Use the techniques from Chapters 4, 5, and 6 to help them learn to recognize and understand their mistake. Eventually, they should be able to do this on their own.

4. Help them think of ways they can behave differently next time.

5. Punish them, if necessary.

6. Let them know you understand they have learned their lesson.

Here is one important caveat about mistakes: Some boys, even good ones, make *huge* mistakes. For example, a very good, smart boy is capable of building a dry ice bomb and detonating it on school grounds. If your boy makes one of these types of mistakes, make note of the following three steps:

1. Determine if it is a pattern of bad behavior for your son. If it is, get him professional help.

2. If it is out of character for your son, the six steps above should still work.

3. Hire a good criminal defense attorney.[209]

I just made a mistake: I totally freaked out on someone in front of my son

This is an area where modeling comes into play. The goal is for you to model appropriate behavior for your boys. They will see you recognizing your emotions and controlling them, and they will learn from you. But there will invariably be times when you mess up, so you must figure out how to handle it when you do.

Believe it or not, a major mess-up is another good opportunity for modeling appropriate behavior. Explain to your boys that you made a mistake. Explain what you did wrong. Explain how you were feeling at the time. Describe to them what you could have done to react more appropriately in the moment. Then tell them how important it is to remember that no one is perfect—everyone is going to make mistakes. The key to mistakes is learning from them so that you don't make them again. Tell your boys what you have learned and how you will act differently next time.

Properly acknowledging and admitting your mistakes sends a powerful message to your boys, and it helps them understand how to gracefully handle their own future mistakes.

It can be especially powerful if you model appropriate apologies to your sons.[210] If you get a chance, say you are sorry to the person with whom you were angry, and let your boys see you do it. If the person is not around, explain to your boys how you would like to apologize to the person if you ever get the chance.

---

[209] I am not kidding about this. If your otherwise good son makes a major mistake, a defense attorney can help a judge understand why your boy is different from the repeat offenders the judge typically sees every day. The attorney can help your son get a lighter punishment.

[210] Hoffman (1975)

In case you are at a loss for words when you are trying to apologize, the following four steps, published in the Journal of Peace Psychology,[211] are fairly effective:[212]

1. Express your emotions in your apology ("I feel *sad* and *embarrassed* that I called you a flaming douche nozzle.").

2. Admit fault ("It was my fault").

3. Say "I apologize" or "I'm sorry." People won't perceive it as a good apology if you don't use those words.

4. Try to explain your behavior, but don't use it as an excuse ("I was really frustrated because of the bad traffic, and I took it out on you. That wasn't fair").

> **TIP #088:** When you make a mistake, admit it to your boys and explain how you will improve next time.

> **TIP #089:** Apologize if you can. If you can't, tell your boys what you would have liked to say if you had the chance.

As an interesting side note, if you teach your boys to be more empathic, they will be more willing to accept apologies from others.[213] Thus, they are less likely to become angry or lose control of their emotions when someone does them wrong.

> **TIP #090:** Teach your boys to be empathic. That will make it easier for them to accept apologies from others.

---

211 Yes, there is a peer-reviewed publication called The Journal of Peace Psychology.
212 Kirchhoff, et al. (2012)
213 McCullough, et al. (1998)

I am having trouble teaching my son how to be less sad (or angry, or scared, etc), because I think he has a good, rational reason for feeling that way

This is an important issue to discuss. There are highly irrational reasons to get angry, such as someone cutting you off in traffic. But there are also good, reasonable times to get angry. Imagine a scenario where your son comes home from school fuming mad. You ask him why he feels that way, and he tells you that on the way home, the school bully punched his friend in the stomach and stole his bike. Are you going to tell your son that his anger is irrational in that scenario? Are you going to tell him the underlying beliefs that people should be nice to each other and not steal are flawed and that is what led to his poor showing of anger?

I hope not. That is a perfectly reasonable time to be angry. The same can be said of sadness or many other seemingly negative and otherwise irrational emotions.

So it is important to help your son understand what to do when his negative emotion is justified. You can't give your son the go-ahead to freak out. You can't tell him to go find that little brat and punch him twice as hard as he punched your friend, even though that might be satisfying in the short-term. You can't just ignore your son either. You have to do something.

The best advice in cases such as these is to encourage your son to feel his emotions without acting out. Listen to him vent anger or frustration, and let him know you understand how he feels. Be supportive. In many cases, you don't even need to offer advice, you just need to listen with empathy. Explain to him that it makes perfect sense that he is upset, but he needs to know that acting out because of his anger is not appropriate. Talk with him about more productive solutions.

TIP #091: If your son is experiencing a rational negative emotion, use your empathy skills to help him express his emotions without acting out on them in an irrational manner. Instead, help him devise a better way of dealing with problematic situations and emotions.

Teaching my boy the techniques in this book is not working because my parenting partner is not willing to help

This is a tricky scenario. You are convinced that the ideas in this book will help improve the lives of your sons, and will help them leave a positive mark on the world. Your partner is not. He/she thinks it will leave your boys confused. It will turn them into girly boys who are constantly being taken advantage of. It will cause them to grow into something other than real men—who are supposed to be powerful, aggressive, and independent. Perhaps your partner just doesn't care. He/she is merely unwilling to help teach your sons to think reflectively, to have empathy, and to control their emotions. What do you do in situations like these?

Before you read any further, let me clarify what I mean by *partner*. Most people have someone in their lives who help them raise their children: grandparents, stepparents, siblings, daycare providers, husbands, wives, and friends, to name a few. All of these people can be considered parenting partners, especially if they take an active role in raising your boys. So for the remainder of this section, when you see the word *partner*, don't think of a romantic partner or significant other—think of a *parenting partner*.

In the psychological research, partners working together to raise a child is referred to as *coparenting*. In general, *good* coparenting is demonstrated through cooperation and agreement. On the other hand, the hallmarks of *problematic* coparenting are conflict and triangulation.[214]

It is important to understand the power of coparenting. When partners are working together as a unified team, their children will be well-adjusted. Children of cooperative parents have fewer behavioral problems, better social skills, and healthier attachments to both parents.[215]

Another important aspect of cooperating as parents is that it will often lead to happier marriages.[216] In a study from 2012, researchers discovered that couples who cooperated in their parenting practices had higher marital satisfaction. Interestingly, this finding was stronger for parents of boys than for parents of girls.[217]

So it is important for you and your partner to be on the same page when it comes to raising your boys. In fact, one common feature among families with delinquent children is that poor communication permeates the household,[218] and communication is the key to cooperative parenting. Research confirms that poor communication can lead to poor behavior in children, especially when that poor communication is coupled with *negative* parenting practices, such as using a lot of punishment and very little praise with children.[219] Further, poor parental communication can lead to decreased marital satisfaction, which primes both

---

[214] Triangulation is a phenomenon where one of the parents and the child align together to undermine the other parent's authority. An example of triangulation would be one parent telling the child to ignore the other parent's punishment because it was unfair. This could result in the child aligning strongly with the *fun* parent and ignoring or resenting the *mean* parent.

[215] Teubert & Pinquart (2010)

[216] For those partners who are married, of course.

[217] Pedro, et al. (2012)

[218] Barton, et al. (1988)

[219] Wymbs (2011)

kids and parents to react negatively to one another, as opposed to parents helping their children navigate their difficult emotions.[220]

With all of this in mind, the techniques in this book will probably not work if your parenting partner is not on board. At best, you will be ineffective. At worst, your partner may end up consciously or unconsciously undermining your efforts and setting up a triangulating situation with your boys.

If you think your partner is not cooperating, you should talk with him or her. Explain why it is important to you that your boys learn the techniques in this book, and ask why your partner does not share that opinion. You should remain nonjudgmental and non-aggressive during this conversation. Your partner may have some good reasons for feeling the way he or she does, but those reasons won't come out if you are in attack mode.

> **TIP #092:** If your partner isn't cooperating, talk about it in a non-aggressive manner.

If it turns out your partner is purposefully undermining your work with your boys, that is a very bad sign. It is not so bad that he or she disagrees with you about how to raise your sons—it is the *manner* in which your partner goes about that disagreement that matters. By avoiding communication with you and actively working to undo what you are trying, your partner is telling you he or she does not respect you or your ideas and does not have the communication skills to work out differences the two of you have.

In severe cases like this, you must think about the long-term health of your relationship and your ability to coparent with your partner. Again, I am not trying to say that your partner has to agree with the techniques in this book or else your relationship and your boys are doomed. But you and your partner *must* agree on how to raise your boys and *must* be able to communicate about differences of opinion. If you are unable to do this, couples

---

[220] Kerig, et al. (1993)

or family therapy[221] could be necessary to learn essential communication and coparenting skills. In extreme cases, you might need to think about the viability of your relationship.

> **TIP #093:** If you can't communicate with your partner, or if your partner is actively working against you, you might benefit from couples or family counseling.

My boys are telling me they are sick of hearing me talk about this stuff

This is a simple one. Just stop talking about it so much. You might be overdoing it. Give your boys a break.

> **TIP #094:** When your boys are telling you to shut up about their emotions, you might be talking about them too much. Take a little time off.

I'm afraid I'm not doing it perfectly: It is too hard to remember to teach my boys all of the time, and I miss a lot of opportunities to talk to them

See above section.

> **TIP #095:** Not everything needs to be a teachable moment. Let your boys play video games and wrestle every now and then.

---

[221] You do not have to be in a romantic relationship with someone to see a couples therapist. A good marriage and family therapist can help parenting partners communicate better with one another, regardless of their relationship to one another.

The problem is getting worse and worse, and my son is not responding, no matter what I try

Now, this can be a serious issue. If you are attempting to follow the steps in this or any other book, and your son is not responding to anything, there might be a real problem. But, you also need to keep in mind these techniques will not work immediately. Although you might see some quick changes in your boys, it will take time for these concepts to really sink in. And, when you are working on changing behaviors, old habits sometimes get worse before you see improvement.

Don't give up too soon. But if it has been several weeks and you have not seen any changes, or if the problem has worsened and does not seem to be improving after a month or two, something might be wrong. It might be a medical issue, so it is important to take your son to his pediatrician and explain what is happening. It might also be a mental health issue, so you might need to talk to a therapist or a psychiatrist. Counseling and/or medication might be beneficial.

> **TIP #096:** When nothing is working to control your son, you need to take immediate action. Get him professional help. Take him to his pediatrician for a physical. While you are there, get a referral for a good child therapist or child psychiatrist for a mental health evaluation.

There are a number of potential warning signs that could indicate your son has a mental or physical problem, and a professional can help you evaluate them. Following is a list of symptoms:[222]

---

[222] Keep in mind, if your son displays one of two of these symptoms, it may not be a big deal. If you recognize more than a few in your son, there could be a real problem.

1. He is sad and withdrawn and does not like to spend time with others.

2. He has no friends.

3. He is angry all/most of the time.

4. Once he gets angry, he seems to lose control of his actions. He can't do anything to calm down and the anger needs to run its course.

5. He is verbally or physically aggressive when he is angry.

6. He is having trouble sleeping, or he sleeps more than 12 hours per day.

7. He eats too much, or he does not eat enough.[223]

8. His moods are volatile, and they change rapidly without warning.

9. He is openly defiant to those in authority.

10. He is getting into a lot of trouble at home and school. He may even be breaking the law.

11. He gets into physical fights with peers or threatens and intimidates others.

12. He is cruel to animals.

13. He cries more than usual.

14. He throws too many temper tantrums.[224]

---

[223] Note: most growing boys eat like horses.
[224] Note: Younger boys who are perfectly normal will throw temper tantrums. As they age, these should decrease and eventually stop.

15. His grades are terrible, even though he is smart enough to do well in school.

16. He does not come home when he is supposed to, and he does not tell you what he is doing.

17. You suspect he is using drugs or alcohol.[225]

18. He is overly stressed much of the time: He panics. He chews his nails. He shakes, cries, paces, and worries.

19. He has difficulty focusing or paying attention.

20. He can't sit still.

21. He has way too much energy.

22. He starts behaving in weird ways: He gets paranoid. He talks to himself. He has very strange thoughts. He misinterprets reality.

23. He stops taking care of his personal hygiene.[226]

24. He complains of hallucinations. (Seeing and hearing things can be a symptom of mental illness. Smelling things that do not exist can be a symptom of several different physical ailments.)

25. He is highly impulsive.

26. He loses interest in activities he used to enjoy.[227]

---

[225] Sometimes drug or alcohol use is just that—a substance use problem. Other times, substance use is masking a deeper problem, as people often use drugs or alcohol to try to take away emotional pain.

[226] Note: Most growing boys smell. Badly.

[227] Note: All boys go through phases, and they grow in and out of interests. But if it seems like your son is losing interest in everything, that can be a problem.

27. He has no motivation to complete tasks.

28. He starts several projects and never finishes them.

29. He drops his friends and starts hanging out with the wrong crowd.

30. He seems physically ill much of the time.

CHAPTER 8

Boys Will Be Boys: conclusion[228]

The turtle. I learned an enormous lesson from its death, and I have tried to impart some of the wisdom I gained from its demise in this book. I hope I have at least partially succeeded.

Of course, it didn't have to die for me to understand the power of recognizing my emotions, regulating them, and having empathy for others. And that is one of the main goals of this book—to stop trying to learn from tragedies and instead to develop ways of avoiding them in the first place. To allow *boys to be boys*. To let them be *all boy*. To encourage them to live full and rewarding lives, unfettered by the old idea that men need to be cold, calculating, and unemotional.

As a parting thought, let me propose something radical: The real moral of the story from Chapter 1 is not to learn how to have

---

[228] Ah, the conclusion chapter of a self-help book. Could there be any chapter that is more useless? If you have read the entire book, with all of its justification, tips, and summaries of the research, what more could you possibly gain from concluding remarks? Yet it seems weird to just end the book abruptly. Let's make a deal—allow me to make one last important point, and I promise to be brief.

empathy for the turtle. Instead, the moral is to learn to have empathy for its killers.

Compassion and sympathy are appropriate for the turtle. In comparison, empathy for the turtle does not seem all that important. At the very least, it is not difficult. Any decent human being can understand what that poor turtle must have been going through in its final moments on earth. That is easy. Sad, but easy.

What is hard is having empathy for the boys who harmed the turtle. Understanding where they were coming from, what they were thinking and feeling, and why they did what they did—that is not an easy task. And it does not require sympathy. There is no need to share their feelings. It does not require compassion, either. There is potentially no need to feel sorry for whatever misfortune had befallen them in their lives. But the intellectual task of empathizing with them—*that* is the challenge. That is what will help your boys be *all boy, a*nd that is what can prevent tragedies from happening in the first place.

Personally and professionally, I believe wholeheartedly that the intellectual pursuit of emotional understanding can transform our society. Teaching our boys to understand their own and others' emotions will give them a tremendously positive life. They will have better friends, happier relationships, and more success in school and work. They will be more effective in negotiations, and they will be more assertive. They will fight for what is right, and they will treat others with kindness and respect—even when those others have done terrible things. In short, they will be strong individuals, poised to change the world. By contrast, another generation of boys who are taught to be aggressive, unemotional, and angry will get left behind. By teaching our boys emotional regulation and empathy, we will open their lives to the full richness of humanity—we will truly *let them be boys.*

As I wrote in the introduction to this book, it occurred to me that there were actions I could have taken as a child to avoid the turtle's death. By better understanding my own emotions, giving myself permission to feel those emotions, and understanding where the other boys were coming from, I could have handled the situation better. I could have stepped up to the conflict and approached the mean boys in an empathic fashion. There was no need to show compassion or sympathy. I didn't need to feel sorry for them or give them a free pass. But I needed to understand where they were coming from. The turtle might not have died, and I would have felt powerful. I could have taken charge of the situation, dealt with the other boys in an assertive and effective manner, and modeled appropriate behavior to my peers. I could have attracted the right kind of friends. I could have been less anxious. I would have been mighty.

Whereas compassion is crucial in helping those who have terrible things happen to them, empathy can lower the number of terrible things that happen. It can lessen the chances of misunderstanding. It can keep a kid from bringing a gun to school. It can encourage society's boys to strive toward peaceful solutions to the world's problems. It can push countries away from war, and it can demand that nations treat each other fairly. It can create a new generation of powerful, confident, effective men.

Empathy truly can change the world—one boy at a time.

REFERENCES

Chapter 1:

Barry, R. A., & Kochanska, G. (2010). A longitudinal investigation of the affective environment in families with young children: From infancy to early school age. *Emotion, 10*(2), 237-249.

Cooper, A., & Smith, E. L. (2011). *Homicide Trends in the United States, 1980-2008, Annual Rates for 2009 and 2010.* U.S. Department of Justice, Bureau of Justice Statistics, November, 2011.

Hartnett, J. & Shumate, M. (1980). Ethical attitudes and moral maturity among prison inmates. *Journal of Psychology: Interdisciplinary and Applied, 106*(1), 147-149.

Kahn, R. E., Byrd, A. L., & Pardini, D. A. (2013). Callous-unemotional traits robustly predict future criminal offending in young men. *Law and Human Behavior, 37*(2), 87-97.

Lucia, S., & Killias, M. (2011). Is animal cruelty a marker of inter-personal violence and delinquency? Results of a Swiss National Self-Report study. *Psychology of Violence, 1*(2), 93-105.

Mackinnon, D. G. (1988). Assessment of maturity in young offenders with the MMPI-A and A-con scales. *Dissertation Abstracts International: Section B: The Sciences and Engineering, 59*(1-B), pp. 442.

Maiuro, R. D., Cahn, T. S., Vitaliano, P. P., Wagner, B. C., & Zegree, J. B. (1988). Anger, hostility, and depression in domestically violent versus generally assaultive men and non-violent control subjects. *Journal of Consulting and Clinical Psychology, 56*(1), 17-23.

National Safety Council (2013). *Injury Facts: 2013 Edition.*

Planty, M., & Langton, L. (2013). *Female Victims of Sexual Violence, 1994-2010.* U.S. Department of Justice, Bureau of Justice Statistics, March, 2013.

Truman, J. L., & Rand, M. R. (2010). *Criminal Victimization, 2009.* U. S. Department of Justice, Bureau of Justice Statistics, October, 2010.

Van Kleef, G. A., Gerben, A., Homan, A. C., Finkenauer, C., Gündemir, S., & Stamkou, E. (2011). Breaking the rules to rise to power: How norm violators gain power in the eyes of others. *Social Psychological and Personality Science, 2*(5), 500-507.

Van Kleef, G. A., Gerben, A., Homan, A. C., Finkenauer, C., Blaker, N. M., & Heerdink, M. W. (2012). Prosocial norm violations fuel power affordance. *Journal of Experimental Social Psychology, 48*(4), 937-942.

Wolchover, N. (2012). Why is everyone on the internet so angry? *Scientific American, July 25, 2012.*

Chapter 2:

Anderson, C. A., Benjamin, A. J., & Bartholow, B. D. (1998). Does the gun pull the trigger? Automatic priming effects of weapon pictures and weapon names. *Psychological Science, 9*(4), 308-314.

Bandura, A. (1965). Influence of a models' reinforcement contingencies on the acquisition of imitative responses. *Journal of Personality and Social Psychology, 1*(6), 589-595.

Bandura, A., Ross, D., & Ross, S. A. (1961). Transmission of aggression through the imitation of aggressive models. *Journal of Abnormal and Social Psychology, 63,* 575-582

Bandura, A., Ross, D., & Ross, S. A. (1963). Imitation of film-mediated aggressive models. *Journal of Abnormal and Social Psychology, 66*(1), 3-11.

Bartholow, B. D., & Anderson, C. A., Carnagey, N. L., Benjamin, A. J. (2005). Interactive effects of life experience and situational cues on aggression: The weapons priming effect in hunters and nonhunters. *Journal of Experimental Social Psychology, 41*(1), 48-60.

Berkowitz, L., & LePage, A. (1967). Weapons as aggression-eliciting stimuli. *Journal of Personality and Social Psychology, 7*(2-1), 202-207.

Brodzinksy, D. M., Messer, S. B., & Tew, J. D. (1979). Sex differences in children's expression and control of fantasy and overt aggression. *Child Development, 50*(2), 372-379.

Butler-Barnes, S. T., Chavous, T. M., & Zimmerman, M. A. (2011). Exposure to violence and achievement motivation beliefs: Moderating roles of cultural-ecological factors. *Race and Social Problems, 3*(2), 75-91.

Copeland, T. V. (1995). The relationship of Protestant fundamentalism and intellectual and moral development among college students. *Dissertation Abstracts International: Section A: Humanities and Social Sciences, 56*(1-A), pp. 0141.

Crownover, C. A. (2011). Faith development, religious fundamentalism, right-wing authoritarianism, social dominance orientation, Christian orthodoxy, and proscribed prejudice as predictors of prejudice. *Dissertation Abstracts International: ection B: The Sciences and Engineering, 68*(4-B), pp. 2711.

Dijkstra, J. K., Lindenberg, S., Veenstra, R., Steglich, C., Issacs, J., Card, N. A., & Hodges, E. V. E. (2010). Influence and selection processes in weapon carrying during adolescence: The roles of status, aggression, and vulnerability. *Criminology: An Interdisciplinary Journal, 48*(1), 187-220.

Eron, L. D. (1980). Prescription for reduction of aggression. *American Psychologist, 35*(3), 244-252.

Farr, R. H., & Patterson, C. J. (2013). Lesbian and gay adoptive parents and their children. In *LGDT-Parent Families: Innovations in Research and Implications For Practice,* Goldberg, A. B., Allen, K. R. (Eds.), New York: Springer Science and Business Media, 39-55.

Florsheim, P., Tolan, P., & Gorman-Smith, D. (1998). Family relationships, parenting practices, the availability of male family members, and the behavior of inner-city boys in single-mother and two-parent families. *Child Development,* 69(5), 1437-1447.

Garo, M. L. (2006). The impact of Christian fundamentalism on adolescent and young adult development: A exploratory qualitative study. *Dissertations Abstracts International: Section B: The Sciences and Engineering,* 67(1), pp. 576.

Garside, R. B., & Klimes-Dougan, B. (2002). Socialization of discrete negative emotions: Gender differences and links with psychological distress, *Sex Roles,* 47(3-4), 115-128.

Golombok, S., & Tasker, F. (1994). Children in lesbian and gay families: Theories and evidence, *Annual Review of Sex Research, V,* 73-100.

Grubb, A., & Turner, E. (2012). Attribution of blame in rape cases: A review of the impact of rape myth acceptance, gender role conformity and substance use on victim blaming. *Aggression and Violent Behavior,* July 7, 2012.

Hardy, M. S., Armstrong, F. D., Martin, B. L., & Strawn, K. N. (1996). A firearm safety program for children: They just can't say no. *Journal of Developmental and Behavioral Pediatrics,* 17(4), 216-221.

Hay, D. F., Nash, A., Caplan, M., Ishikawa, F., & Vespo, J. E. (2011). The emergence of gender differences in physical aggression in the context of conflict between young peers. *British Journal of Developmental Psychology,* 29(2), 158-175.

Himle, M. B., Miltenberger, R. G., Flessner, C., & Gatheridge, B. (2004). Teaching safety skills to children to prevent gun play. *Journal of Applied Behavior Analysis, 37*(1), 1-9.

Kim, S., Miles-Mason, E., Kim, C. K., & Esquivel, G. B. (2012). Religiosity/spirituality and life satisfaction in Korean American adolescents. *Psychology of Religion and Spirituality*, Dec. 31, 2012.

Klimes-Dougan, B., Brand, A. E., Zahn-Waxler, C., Hastings, P. D., & Garside, R. B. (2007). Parental emotion socialization in adolescence: Differences in sex, age, and problem status. *Social Development, 16*(2), 326-342.

Klinesmith, J., Kasser, T., & McAndrew, F. T. (2006). Guns, testosterone, and aggression: An experimental test of a meditational hypothesis. *Psychological Science, 17*(7), 568-571.

Knox, M., Burkhart, K., & Khuder, S. A. (2011). Parental hostility and depression and predictors of young children's aggression and conduct problems. *Journal of Aggression, Maltreatment and Trauma, 20*(7), 800-811.

LeBlanc, G. (2008). A developmental-ecological perspective on the role of spirituality in the development of meaningfulness in adolescent boys. *Research in the Social Scientific Study of Religion, 19*, 255-277.

Liu, J., Portnoy, J., & Raine, A. (2012). Association between a marker for prenatal testosterone exposure and externalizing behavior problems in children. *Development and Psychopathology, 24*(3), 771-782.

MacCallum, F., & Golombok, S. (2004). Children raised in fatherless families from infancy: A Follow-up of children of lesbian and single heterosexual mothers at early adolescence. *Journal of Child Psychology and Psychiatry, 45*(8), 1407-1419.

MacCallum, F., Tasker, F., & Murray, C. (1997). Children raised in fatherless families from infancy: Family relationships and the socioemotional development of children of lesbian and single heterosexual mothers. *Journal of Child Psychology and Psychiatry, 38*(7), 783-791.

Mae, L. (2001). Boomerange effects of bigoted speech. *Dissertation Abstracts International: Section B: The Sciences and Engineering, 62*(6-B), pp. 2291.

Meyer, G., Roberto, A. J., & Atkin, C. K. (2003). A radio-based approach to promoting gun safety: Process and outcome evaluation implications and insights. *Health Communication, 15*(3), 299-318.

Miltenberger, R. G., Gatheridge, B. J., Satterlund, M., Egemo-Helm, K. R., Johnson, B. M., Jostad, C., Kelso, P., Flessner, C. A. (2005). Teaching safety skills to children to prevent gun play: An evaluation of in situ training. *Journal of Applied Behavior Analysis, 3*(3), 395-398.

Mokrue, K., Chen, Y. Y., & Elias, M. (2012). The interaction between family structure and child gender on behavior problems in urban ethnic minority children. *International Journal of Behavioral Development, 36*(2), 130-136.

Nagtegaal, M. H., Rassin, E., & Muris, P. E. H. M. (2009). Do members of shooting associations display higher levels of aggression? *Psychology, Crime Law, 15*(4), 313-325.

Panak, W. F., & Garber, J. (1992). Role of aggression, rejection, and attributions in the prediction of depression in children. *Development and Psychopathology, 4*(1), 145-165.

Peterson, C. K., & Harmon-Jones, E. (2012). Anger and testosterone: Evidence that situationally-induced anger relates to situationally-induced testosterone. *Emotion, 12*(5), 899-902.

Rice, S., Hackett, H., Trafimow, D., Hunt, G., Sandry, J. (2012). Damned if you do and damned if you don't: Assigning blame to victims regardless of their choice. *The Social Science Journal, 49*(1), 5-8.

Rudolph, J. W. (2004). Into the big muddy and out again: Error persistence and crisis management in the operating room.

Dissertation Abstracts International. B. The Sciences and Engineering, 64(8-b), 4079.

Sher, L. (2012). Testosterone and suicidal behavior. *Expert Review of Neurotherapeutics, 12*(3), 257-259.

Sher, l., Grunebaum, M. F., Sullivan, G. M., Burke, A. K., Cooper, T. B., Mann, J. J., & Oquendo, M. A. (2012). Testosterone levels in suicide attempters with bipolar disorder. *Journal of Psychiatric Research, 46*(10), 1267-1271.

Wan, L. C., Chan, E. K. Y., & Su, L. (2011). When will customers care about service failures that happened to strangers? The role of personal similarity and regulatory focus and its implication on service evaluation. *International Journal of Hospitality Management, 30*(1), 213-220.

Watson, M. W., & Peng, Y. (1992). The relation between toy gun play and children's aggressive behavior. *Early Education and Development, 3*(4), 370-389.

Willoughby, T., Adachi, P. J. C., & Good, M. (2012). A longitudinal study of the association between violent video game play and aggression among adolescents. *Developmental Psychology, 48*(4), 1044-1057.

Yildirim, B. O., & Derksen, J. J. L. (2012). A review on the relationship between testosterone and life-course persistent antisocial behavior. *Psychiatry Research, August 24, 2012.*

Chapter 2.5:

American Psychiatric Association (2013). *Diagnostic and Statistical Manual of Mental Disorders, Fifth Edition (DSM-5)*, American Psychiatric Association, Arlington, VA.

Breithaupt, F. (2012). Author reply: Empathy does provide rational support for decisions. But, is it the right decision? *Emotion Review, 4*(1), 96-97.

Cho, S. Y., & Min, K-H. (2011). Who makes utilitarian judgments? The influences of emotions on utilitarian judgments. *Judgment and Decision Making, 6*(7), 580-592.

Johnson, J. D., Simmons, C. H., Jordan, A., MacLean, L., Taddei, J., Thomas, D., Dovido, J. F., Reed, W. (2002). Rodney King and O. J. revisited: The impact of race and defendant empathy induction on judicial decisions. *Journal of Applied Social Psychology, 32*(6), 1208-1223.

Chapter 3:

Ang, R. P., & Goh, D. H. (2010). Cyberbullying among adolescents: The role of affective and cognitive empathy, and gender. *Child Psychiatry and Human Development, 41*(4), 387-397.

Belacchi, C., & Farina, E. (2012). Feeling and thinking of others: Affective and cognitive empathy and emotion comprehension in prosocial/hostile preschoolers. *Aggressive Behavior, 38*(2), 150-165.

Chapman, C., & Musselwhite, C. B. A. (2011). Equine road user safety: Public attitudes, understandings and beliefs from a qualitative study in the United Kingdom. *Accident Analysis and Prevention, 43*(6), 2173-2181.

Chunharas, A., Hetrakul, P., Boonyobol, R., Udomkitti, T., Tassanapitkul, T., & Wattanasirichaigoon, D. (2013). Medical students themselves as surrogate patients increased satisfaction, confidence, and performance in practicing injection skill. *Medical Teacher, 35*(4), 308-313.

Cordier, R., Bundy, A., Hocking, C., & Einfeld, S. (2010). Empathy in the play of children with attention deficit hyperactivity disorder. *OTJR: Occupation, Participation and Health, 30*(3), 122-132.

de Wied, M., Branje, S. J. T., & Meeus, W. H. J. (2007). Empathy and conflict resolution in friendship relations among adolescents. *Aggressive Behavior, 33*(1), 48-55.

de Wied, M., Goudena, P. P., & Matthys, W. (2005). Empathy in boys with disruptive behavior disorders. *Journal of Child Psychology and Psychiatry, 46*(8), 867-880.

de Wied, M., van Boxtel, A., Zaalberg, R., Goudena, P. P., Matthys, W. (2006). Facial EMG responses to dynamic emotional facial expression in boys with disruptive behavior disorders. *Journal of Psychiatric Research, 40*(2), 112-121.

Derntl, B., Seidel, E. M., Schneider, F., & Habel, U. (2012). How specific are emotional deficits? A comparison of empathic abilities in schizophrenia, bipolar and depressed patients. *Schizophrenia Research, 142*(1-3), 58-64.

Eisenberg, N., Losoya, S., Fabes, R. A., Guthrie, I. K., Reiser, M., Murphy, B., Shepard, S. A., Poulin, R., & Padgett, S. J. (2001). Parental socialization of children's dysregulated expression of emotion and externalizing problems. *Journal of Family Psychology, 15*(2), 183-205.

Elbers, N. A., van Wees, K. A. P. C., Akkermans, A. J., Cuijpers, P., & Bruinvels, D. J. (2012). Exploring lawyer-client interaction: A qualitative study of positive lawyer characteristics. *Psychology Injury and Law, 5*(1), 89-94.

Foa, U. G. (1956). A test of the foremanworker relationship. *Personnel Psychology, 9,* 469-486.

Frankl, V. (2006). *Man's Search For Meaning,* New York: Beacon Press, pp. 184.

Garner, P. W., & Waajid, B. (2008). The associations of emotion knowledge and teacher-child relationships to preschool children's school-related developmental competence. *Journal of Applied Developmental Psychology, 29*(2), 89-100.

Gleason, K. A. (2005). The effects of empathic accuracy on childhood relationships. *Dissertation Abstracts International: Section B: The Sciences and Engineering, 65*(9-B), pp. 4869.

Hirvela, S., & Helkama, K. (2011). Empathy, values, morality and Asperger's syndrome. *Scandanavian Journal of Psychology, 52*(6), 560-572.

Hojat, M., Gonnella, J. S., Mangione, S., Nasca, T. J., Veloski, J. J., Erdman, J. B., Callahan, C. A., Magee, M. (2002). Empathy in medical students as related to academic performance, clinical competence and gender. *Medical Education, 36*(6), 522-527.

Holt, S., & Marques, J. (2012). Empathy in leadership: Appropriate or misplaced? An empirical study on a topic that is asking for attention. *Journal of Business Ethics, 105*(1), 95-105.

Jagers, R. J., Sydnor, K., Mouttapa, M., & Flay, B. R. (2007). Protective factors associated with preadolescent violence: Preliminary work on a cultural model. *American Journal of Community Psychology, 40*(1-2), 138-145.

Li, Y., Lynch, A. D., Kalvin, C., Liu, J., & Lerner, R. M. (2011). Peer relationships as a context for the development of school engagement during early adolescence. *International Journal of Behavioral Development, 35*(4), 329-342.

London, M., Fuchs, N., Oddo, J., & Williams, D. (2013). Counselor effectiveness in a summer camp for HIV youth. *34th Annual Meeting and Scientific Sessions of the Society of Behavioral Medicine, March 20-23-, 2013, San Francisco, CA.*

Mariana, S. (2013). Correctional counselor relational competency assessment: Development and validation. *Dissertation Abstracts International: Section B: The Sciences and Engineering, 73*(8-B(e)), no pagination specified.

Marsh, P., Beauchaine, T. P., & Williams, B. (2008). Dissociation of sad facial expressions and autonomic nervous system responding in boys with disruptive behavior disorders. *Psychophysiology, 45*(1), 100-110.

Marton, I. (2009). Social perspective taking, empathy and social outcomes in children with Attention-Deficit/Hyperactivity Disorder. *Dissertation Abstracts International: Section B: The Sciences and Engineering, 69*(12-B), pp. 7818.

Mavroveli, S., & Sánchez-Ruiz, M. J. (2011). Trait emotional intelligence influences on academic achievement and school behaviour. *British Journal of Educational Psychology, 81*(1), 112-134.

Miley, W. M., & Spinella, M. (2007). Correlations among executive function scales and positive psychological attributes in college students. *Psychological Reports, 100*(1), 24-26.

Natale, S. M., & Sora, S. A. (2010). Ethics in strategic thinking: Business processes and the global market collapse. *Journal of Business Ethics, 94*(3), 309-316.

Negd, M., Mallan, K. M., & Lipp, O. V. (2011). The role of anxiety and perspective-taking strategy on affective empathic responses. *Behaviour Research and Therapy, 49*(12), 852-857.

Nordstrom, K., & Korpelainene, P. (2011). Creativity and inspiration for problem solving in engineering education. *Teaching in Higher Education, 16*(4), 439-450.

Puskar, A. (2012). Investigating the relationship between the cognitive and affective components of empathy and frontal lobe functioning in college students. *Dissertation Abstracts International: Section B: The Sciences and Engineering, 7*(9-B), pp. 5579.

Szyper-Perl, S. (1969). Approach to the behavior dynamics of salesmen and investigation of empathy as a personality variable in a battery of tests. *Bulletin du C.E.R.P., 18*(1), 65-78.

Thoma, P., Zalewski, I., von Reventlow, H. G., Norra, C., Juckel, G., & Daum, I. (2011). Cognitive and affective empathy in depression linked to executive control. *Psychiatry Research, 189*(3), 373-378.

Totan, T., Dogan, T., & Sapmaz, F. (2013). Emotional self-efficacy, emotional empathy and emotional approach coping as sources of happiness. *Cypriot Journal of Educational Sciences, 8*(2), 247-256.

Tullett, A., Placks, J., & Tackett, J. (2013). An incremental theory of happiness predicts empathic responding. *3rd Biennial Conference of the Association for Research in Personality, June 20-22, 2013, Charlotte, NC.*

Uekermann, J., Kraemer, M., Abdel-Hamid, M., Schimmelmann, B. G., Hebebrand, J., Daum, I., Wiltfang, J., & Kis, B. (2010). Social cognition in attention-deficit hyperactivity disorder (ADHD). *Neuroscience and Biobehavioral Reviews, 35*(5), 734-743.

Vaziri, S. A., & Afsaneh, L. (2012). The effect of empathy training in decreasing adolescents' aggression. *Journal of Iranian Psychologists, 8*(30), 167-176.

Verbeek, P. (1997). Peacemaking of young children. *Dissertation Abstracts International: Section B: The Sciences and Engineering, 57*(11-B), pp. 7253.

Wang, F. M., Chen, J. Q, Xiao, W. Q., Ma, Y. T., & Zhang, M. (2012). Peer physical aggression and its association with aggressive beliefs, empathy, self-control, and cooperation skills among students in a rural town in China. *Journal of Interpersonal Violence, 27*(16), 3252-3267.

Warren, M. A. (2004). Parent-child interactions with ADHD children: Parental empathy as a predictor of child adjustment. *Dissertation Abstracts International: Section B: The Sciences and Engineering, 64*(9-B), pp. 4658.

Way, N., & Silverman, L. R. (2012). The quality of friendships during adolescence: Patterns across context, culture, and age. In *Adolescence and beyond: Family processes and development. Kerig, P. K., Schulz, M. A., Hauser, S. T. (eds.),* 91-112. New York: Oxford University Press.

Wei, M., Liao, K. Y., Ku, T., & Shaffer, P. A. (2011). Attachment, self-compassion, empathy, and subjective well-being among college students and community adults. *Journal of Personality, 79*(1), 191-221.

Wyatt, J. M. (2002). An outcome evaluation of an after-school program for children with emotional and behavioral disorders. *Dissertations Abstracts International: Section B; The Sciences and Engineering, 63*(6-B), pp. 3048.

Yeo, L. S., Ang, R. P., Loh, S., Fu, K. J., & Karre, J. K. (2011). The role of affective and cognitive empathy in physical, verbal, and indirect aggression of a Singaporean sample of boys. *Journal of Psychology: Interdisciplinary and Applied, 145*(4), 313-330.

Zienkewicz, L. H. (2010). Student intrinsic strengths: Role in success in community college online and face-to-face courses. *Dissertation Abstracts International: Section A: Humanities and Social Sciences, 71*(1-A), pp. 124.

Chapter 4:

Beck, A. (1976). Cognitive therapy and the emotional disorders. New York: International University Press.

Blom-Hoffman, J. (2001). Intervening in dietary habits of African-American children: An impact evaluation of the every day, lots of ways interdisciplinary nutrition education curriculum. *Dissertation Abstracts International: Section B: The Sciences and Engineering, 62*(4-B), pp. 2043.

Boudreau, E., & D'Entremont, B. (2010). Improving the pretend play skills of preschoolers with autism spectrum disorders: The effects of video modeling. *Journal of Developmental and Physical Disabilities, 22*(4), 415-431.

Buzzetta, C. A. (2012). Family conflict: The adolescent experience of parent-adolescent conflict and argument. *Dissertation Abstracts International, Section A: Humanities and Social Sciences, 73*(5-A), pp. 1935.

Calpin, J. P., & Cinciripini, P. M. (1980). A multiple baseline analysis of social skills training in children. *Corrective Social Pyschiatry Journal of Behavioral Technology, Methods, Therapy, 26*(4), 172-178.

Chan, T., Kyere, K., Davis, B. R., Shemyakin, A., Kabitzke, P. A., Shair, H. N., Barr, G. A., & Wiedenmayer, C. P. (2011). The role of the medial prefrontal cortex in innate fear regulation in infants, juveniles, and adolescents. *The Journal of Neuroscience, 31*(13), 4991-4999.

Davidson-Williams, C. M. (1997). Case study of the mandatory enforcement of a voluntary student uniform policy. *Dissertation Abstracts International, Section A: Humanities and Social Sciences, 57*(10-A), pp. 4199.

DiLorenzo, T., Stucky-Ropp, R. C., Vandel Wal, J. S. & Gotham, H. J. (1998). Determinants of exercise among children: II. A longitudinal study. *Preventive Medicine: An International Journal Devoted to Practice and Theory, 27*(3), 470-477.

Elfhag, K., Tynelius, P., & Rasmussen, F. (2010). Family links of eating behaviour in normal weight and overweight children. *International Journal of Pediatric Obesity, 5*(6), 491-500.

Ellis, A. (1962). Reason and emotion in psychotherapy. New York: L. Stuart.

Ellis, A., & Dryden, W. (1997). The practice of rational emotive behavior therapy, Second Edition. New York: Springer Publishing.

Emotion Words List (n.d.). *UWire for College Students.* From www.wire.wisc.edu/quizzesnmore/emotionwords.aspx.

Engelen, E., Markowitsch, H. J., Scheve, C. v., Röttger-Rössler, B., Stephan, A., Holodynski, M., & Vandekerckhove, M. (2009). Emotions as bio-cultural processes: Disciplinary debates and an interdisciplinary outlook. In Röttger-Rössler, B. (ed.), *Emotions As Bio-Cultural Processes.* New York: Springer Science Business Media, pp. 418.

Fields, B. A. (1989). A classroom-based social skills training program for children with social competence and school adjustment problems. *Journal of Intellectual and Developmental Disability, 15*(2), 99-107.

Fleming, C. B., Brewer, D. D., Gainey, R. R., Haggerty, K. P., & Catalano, R. F. (1997). Parent drug use and bonding to parents as predictors of substance use in children of substance abusers. *Journal of Child Adolescent Substance Abuse, 6*(4), 75-86.

Hay, D. F., Murray, P., Cecire, S., & Nash, A. (1985). Social learning of social behavior in early life. *Child Development, 56*(1), 43-57.

He, M., Piche, L., Beyon, C., & Harris, S. (2010). Screen-related sedentary behaviors: Children's and parents' attitudes, motivations, and practices. *Journal of Nutrition Education, 42*(1), 17-25.

Hermanns, J. M., & De Winthers, P. E. (1971). Observational learning and imitation: A developmental study. *Anthropology and Medicine, 19*(2), 95-108.

King, K. A., Vidourek, R. A., & Wagner, D. I. (2003). Effect of parent drug use and parent-child time spent together on adolescent involvement in alcohol, tobacco, and other drugs. *Adolescent Family Health, 3*(4), 171-176.

Kodl, M. M., & Mermelstein, R. (2004). Beyond modeling: Parenting practices, parental smoking history, and adolescent cigarette smoking. *Addictive Behaviors, 29*(1), 17-32.

Liang, Z., Zhang, G., Chen, H., & Zhang, P. (2012). Relations among parental meta-emotion philosophy, parental emotion expressivity, and children's social competence. *Acta Psychologica Sinica, 44*(2), 199-210.

Matsumoto, D., & Hwang, H. S. (2012). Culture and emotion: The integration of biological and cultural contributions. *Journal of Cross-Cultural Psychology, 43*(1), 91-118.

McGee, R., Williams, S., & Reeder, A. (2006). Parental tobacco smoking behaviour and their children's smoking and cessation in adulthood. *Addiction, 101*(8), 1193-1201.

Morrongiello, B. A., & Mark, L. (2008). 'Practice what you preach': Induced hypocrisy as an intervention strategy to reduce children's intentions to risk take on playgrounds. *Journal of Pediatric Psychology, 33*(10), pp. 1117-1128.

Rayner, C. (2011). Sibling and adult video modeling to teach a student with autism: Imitation skills and intervention suitability. *Developmental Neurorehabilitation, 14*(6), 331-338.

Rhodes, R. E., Naylor, P., & McKay, H. A. (2010). Pilot study of a family physical activity planning intervention among parents and their children.

Schuck, K., Otten, R., Engels, R. C. M. E., & Kleinjan, M. (2012). The role of environmental smoking in smoking-related conditions and susceptibility to smoking in neverosmoking 9-12 year-old children. *Addictive Behaviors, 37*(12), 1400-1405.

Wert, B. Y., & Neisworth, J. T. (2003). Effects of video self-modeling on spontaneous requesting in children with autism. *Journal of Positive Behavior Interventions, 5*(1), 30-34.

Wrotniak, B. H., Epstein, L. H., Paluch, R. A., & Roemmich, J. N. (2005). The relationship between parent and child self-reported adherence and weight loss. *Obesity Research, 13*(6), 1089-1096.

Zimmerman, B. J. (1974). Acquiring and retaining conservation of length through modeling and reversibility cues. *Merrill-Palmer Quarterly, 20*(3), 145-161.

Chapter 5:

Agarwal, P. K., Bain, P. M., & Chamberlain, R. W. (2012). The value of applied research: Retrieval practice improves classroom learning and recommendations from a teacher, a principal, and a scientist. *Educational Psychology Review, 24*(3), 437-448.

Callanan, M. A., & Braswell, G. (2006). Parent-child conversations about science and literacy: Links between formal and informal learning. In *Learning in Places: The Informal Education Reader*. Bekerman, Z., Burbules, N. C., Silberman-Keller, D. (eds.). New York: Peter Lang Publishing, Vol. 249, 2006, pp.123-137.

Carr, M. (2011). Young children reflection on their learning: Teachers' conversation strategies. *Early Years: An*

International Journal of Research and Development, *31*(3), 257-270.

Chen, J. C., Whittinghill, D. C., & Kadlowec, J. A. (2010). Classes that click: Fast, rich feedback to enhance student learning and satisfaction. *Journal of Engineering Education,* *99*(2), 159-168.

Connors, G. J., DiClemente, C. C., Velasquez, M. M., & Donovan, D. M. (2013). Susbtance abuse treatment and the stages of change: Selecting and planning interventions (2nd ed.). New York: Guilford Press.

Ferguson, S. D. (2009). Teacher-leader's use of reflective assessment practices to improve student learning. *Dissertation Abstracts International, Section A: Humanities and Social Sciences, 70*(6-A), pp. 1900.

Jove, G. (2011). How do I improve what I am doing as a teacher, teacher educator and action-researcher through reflection? A learning walk from Lleida to Winchester and back again. *Educational Action Research, 19*(3), 261-278.

Kozminsky, E., & Kozminsky, L. (2002). The dialogue page: Teacher and student dialogues to improve learning motivation. *Intervention in School Clinic, 38*(2), 88-95.

Lenz, K., Graner, P., & Adams, G. (2003). Learning expressways: Building academic relationships to improve learning. *Teaching Exceptional Children, 35*(3), 70-73.

Li, L., Liu, X., & Steckelberg, A. L. (2010). Assessor or assessee: How student learning improves by giving and receiving peer feedback. *British Journal of Educational Technology, 41*(3), 525-536.

Slaughter, V., & Peterson, C. C. (2012). How conversational input shapes theory of mind development in infancy and early childhood. In *Access To Language And Cognitive Development.* Siegel, M., Surian, L. (eds.). New York: Oxford University Press, pp. 3-22.

Strickland, B. S. (2007). Increasing teacher learning to improve student learning. In Lick, D. W., Murphy, C. U. (Eds.) *The Whole-Faculty Study Groups Fieldbook: Lessons Learned And Best Practices From Classrooms, Districts and Schools.* Thousand Oaks: Corwin Press, pp. 303.

Thoonen, E. E. J., Sleegers, P. J. C., Oort, F. J., Peetsma, T. T. D., & Geijsel, F. P. (2011). How to improve teaching practices: The role of teacher motivation, organizational factors, and leadership practices. *Educational Administration Quarterly, 47*(3), 496-536.

Yoder, J. D., & Hochevar, C. M. (2005). Encouraging active learning can improve students' performance on examinations. *Teaching of Psychology, 32*(2), 91-95.

Chapter 6:

I will give you a break from references in Chapter 6. It's a summary chapter, after all.

Chapter 7:

Barton, C., Alexander, J. F., & Turner, C. W. (1988). Defensive communications in normal and delinquent families: The impact of context and family role. *Journal of Family Psychology, 1*(4), 390-405.

Beaver, K. M., Barnes, J. C., May, J. S., & Schwartz, J. A. (2011). Psychopathic personality traits, genetic risk, and gene-environment correlations. *Criminal Justice and Behavior, 38*(9), 896-912.

Benjamin, S., & Taylor, W. D. (2010). Nature and nurture: Genetic influences and gene-environment interactions in depression. *Current Psychiatry Reviews, 6*(2), 82-90.

Bezdijian, S., Baker, L. A., & Tuvblad, C. (2011). Genetic and environmental influences on impulsivity: A meta-analysis of twin, family, and adoption studies. *Clinical Psychology Review*, *31*(7), 1209-1223.

Bleiberg, E. (1988). Adolescence, sense of self, and narcissistic vulnerability. *Bulletin of the Menninger Clinic, 52*(3), 211-228.

Boekholt, M., & des Ligneris, J. (2003). Le narcissisme chez l'enfant: Modalitiés normales et pathologiques / Narcissism in the child: Normal and pathological modalities. *Psychologie Clinique et Projective, 9*, 95-116.

Bornolova, M. A., Blazei, R., Malone, S. H., McGue, M., & Iacono, W. G. (2012). Disentangling the relative contribution of parental antisociality and family discord to child disruptive disorders. *Personality Disorders: Theories, Research, and Treatment, August 13, 2012*, no pagination specified.

Cho, H. J., Meira-Lima, I., Cordeiro, Q., Michelon, L., Sham, P., Vallada, H., & Collier, D. A. (2005). Population-based and family-based studies on the serotonin transporter gene polymorphisms and bipolar disorder: A systematic review and meta-analysis. *Molecular Psychiatry, 10*(8), 771-781.

Dixon, S. V., Graber, J. A., & Brooks-Gunn, J. (2008). The roles of respect for parental authority and parenting practices in parent-child conflict among African American, Latino, and European American families. *Journal of Family Psychology, 22*(1), 1-10.

Edwards, N. A., Sullivan, J. M., Meany-Walen, K., & Kantor, K. (2010). Child parent relationship training: Parents' perceptions of process and outcome. *International Journal of Play Therapy, 19*(3), 159-173.

Harvey, E. A., Metcalfe, L. A., Herbert, S. D., & Fanton, J. H. (2011). The role of family experiences and ADHD in the early development of oppositional defiant disorder. *Journal of Consulting and Clinical Psychology, 79*(6), 784-795.

Hawk, S. T., Keijsers, L., Frijns, T., Hale III, W. W., & Branje, S. (2013). I still haven't found what I'm looking for: Parental privacy invasion predicts reduced parental knowledge. *Developmental Psychology, 49*(7), 1286-1298.

Hawk, S. T., Keijsers, L., Hale III, W. W., & Meeus, W. (2009). Mind your own business! Longitudinal relations between perceived privacy invasion and adolescent-parent conflict. *Journal of Family Psychology, 23*(4), 511-520.

Hettema, J. M., Neal, M. C., & Kendler, K. S. (2001). A review and meta-analysis of the genetic epidemiology of anxiety disorders. *The American Journal of Psychiatry, 158*(10), 1568-1578.

Hicks, B. M., Carlson, M. D., Blonigen, D. M., Patrick, C. J., Iacono, W. G., & MGue, M. (2012). Psychopathic personality traits and environmental contexts: Differential correlates, gender differences, and genetic mediation. *Personality Disorders: Theory, Research, and Treatment, 3*(3), 209-227.

Hoffman, M. L. (1975). Altruistic behavior and the parent-child relationship. *Journal of Personality and Social Psychology, 31*(5), 937-943.

Keijsers, L., & Poulin, F. (2013). Developmental changes in parent-child communication throughout adolescence. *Developmental Psychology,* March 11, 2013, no pagination specified.

Kerig, P. K., Cowan, P. A., & Cowan, C. P. (1993). Marital quality and gender differences in parent-child interaction. *Developmental Psychology, 29*(6), 931-939.

Kirchhoff, J., Wagner, U., & Strack, M. (2012). Apologies: Words of magic? The role of verbal components, anger reduction, and offence severity. *Peace and Conflict: Journal of Peace Psychology, 18*(2), 109-130.

Klahr, A. M., McGue, M., Iacono, W. G., & Burt, A. (2011). The association between parent-child conflict and adolescent conduct problems over time: Results from a longitudinal adoption study. *Journal of Abnormal Psychology, 120*(1), 46-56.

Laursen, B., Pulkkinen, L., & Adams, R. (2002). The antecedents and correlates of agreeableness in adulthood. *Developmental Psychology, 38*(4), 591-603.

Mahler, M. S., Pine, F., & Bergman, A. (1994). Stages in the infant's separation from the mother. In Handel, G., Whitchurch, G. G. (Eds.) *The Psychosocial Interior of the Family (4th ed.)*. Hawthorne, NY: Aldine de Gruyter, pp. 419-448.

McCullough, M. E., Rachal, K. C., Sandage, S. J., Worthington Jr., E. L., Everett, L., Brown, S. W., & Hight, T. L. (1998). Interpersonal forgiving in close relationships: II. Theoretical elaboration and measurement. *Journal of Personality and Social Psychology, 75*(6), 1586-1603.

Pedro, M. F., Ribeiro, T., & Shelton, K. H. (2012). Marital satisfaction and partners' parenting practices: The mediating role of coparenting behavior. *Journal of Family Psychology, 26*(4), 509-522.

Pemment, J. (2013). The neurobiology of antisocial personality disorder: The quest for rehabilitation and treatment. *Aggression and Violent Behavior, 18*(1), 79-82.

Raine, A. (2013). *The Anatomy of Violence: The Biological Roots of Crime*. New York: Pantheon/Random House.

Sadeh, N., Shabnama, J., & Verona, E. (2013). Analysis of monoaminergic genes, childhood abuse, and dimensions of psychopathy. *Journal of Abnormal Psychology, 122*(1), 167-179.

Schlitz, K., Witzel, J. G., & Bogerts (2011). Neurobiological and clinical aspects of violent offenders. *Minerva Psichiatrica, 52*(4), 187-203.

Shippee-Blum, E. V. (1959). The young rebel: Self-regard and ego-ideal. *Journal of Consulting Psychology, 23*(1), 44-50.

Singh, A. L., & Waldman, I. D. (2010). The etiology of associations between negative emotionality and childhood externalizing disorders. *Journal of Abnormal Psychology, 119*(2), 376-388.

Teubert, D., & Pinquart, M. (2010). The association between coparenting and child adjustment: A meta-analysis. *Parenting: Science and Practice, 10*(4), 286-307.

Vidding, E., & McRory, E. J. (2012). Genetic and neurocognitive contributions to the development of psychopathy. *Development and Psychopathology, 24*(3), 969-983.

Wilson, K. R., Havighurst, S. S., & Harley, A. E. (2012). Tuning in to kids: An effectiveness trial of a parenting program targeting emotion socialization of preschoolers. *Journal of Family Psychology, 26*(1), 56-65.

Wymbs, B. T. (2011). Mechanisms underlying the influence of disruptive child behavior on interparental communication. *Journal of Family Psychology, 25*(6), 873-884.

Chapter 8:

No references here. Go have some fun with your boys!

CPSIA information can be obtained at www.ICGtesting.com
Printed in the USA
BVOW05s2011071215

429602BV00002B/45/P